·FATHER·BOB·OGLE·

A MAN OF LETTERS

FATHER · BOB · OGLE

A MAN OF LETTERS

by Father Bob Ogle
O.C, J.C.D., D.D.HON., PH.D.HON.

Broadcasting for International Understanding, Ottawa

Canadian Cataloguing in Publication Data

Ogle, Bob, 1928–
A man of letters

ISBN: 0-9694509-0-7

1. Ogle, Bob, 1928– –Correspondence.
2. Economic assistance, Canadian–Developing countries.
3. Clergy–Canada–Correspondence. I. Broadcasting for International Understanding (Association). II. Title.

FC626.045A4 1990 338.9'17101724 C90-097079-0
F1034.3.045A4 1990

Published by:
Broadcasting for International Understanding

Cover photo: Dark Horse Studios, Saskatoon
Cover and book design: Robert Grey
Typeset in Berkeley Oldstyle Medium by Apex Graphics, Saskatoon
Printed by Gagne Printing, 80 St. Martin Ave., Louisville, Que. J5V 1B4

Dedicated to the memory
of Caroline Heath–
friend, editor, poet–cut down by cancer
in the prime of her life, April 13, 1989.

From the desk of Father Bob . . .

For the past five years, I have lived in a special space. Medical people have told me several times that I have only "a few days left to live."

Such a warning has its advantages. Not only do your priorities change, you also try to put your life in order by doing a bit of housecleaning.

During the summer of 1989 I sorted through almost 10,000 slides, and dispatched photos and paraphernalia to various friends and relatives around the world. One day in my sorting, I came upon a full set of the letters I had written during my year of research with the International Development Research Centre (1975–76). Barbara Armstrong, a friend from book-publishing days, happened by and asked if she could read the letters. The next day she phoned to say, "You have another book here."

Well, the letters were never meant to be a book. But I have learned to "pay attention." I tested the letters on several people including Sister Therese Sullivan, whose doctoral work was in the spiritual interpretation of letters.

Publishers gave half-hearted responses and distant promises, but a brain tumour cannot wait. It was decided to go ahead, form a team, raise the money, have Broadcasting for International Understanding act as publisher, and "do it." Novalis's participation is also much appreciated.

Things began to fall into place and *A Man of Letters,* a name suggested by my sister Mary Lou, became a reality.

Very few people ever have the opportunity to take a 17-month sabbatical in mid-life. Even fewer have a chance to tour the globe, mix around with the folks on several continents, and come out of it unscathed. My problem while on this sabbatical was how I would tell people about my experience.

I decided to send a letter on the first of every month from wherever I was at that particular time. A Saskatoon friend, Arlene Boulanger, would receive the draft, make about 100 copies, and an Ottawa friend, Cecile Poilievre, would send them out to a list of friends and relatives.

Any letter-writing abilities I have came to me honestly from my mother. She was a superb letter writer. One of my earliest recollections is of watching her sitting next to a smoky coal-oil lamp, straight pen in hand, scripting her weekly message to Grandma and relatives "back east." Later, the letters were sent to neighbours and cousin-soldiers all over the world. And finally, to me. In the seminary, at a time when mail service was still accurate and certain, I would wait each Wednesday in London, Ontario, for her Sunday letter from Rosetown, Saskatchewan. Other seminarians gaped at and envied my 8 to 12 page epistles that told of simple things: the new kitchen linoleum, the dog's sore paw, a neighbour's new car. For a while I would be home again in mind and spirit.

But then her disease, one I now share, caught up to her, and there were breaks in her letter writing, and pain in my heart. Her greatest hope was to see me ordained . . . but she died before it happened. She left her disease in my bones, but she also left the notion that writing letters is important.

My experience as a missionary in Brazil in the mid-1960s was a new and shocking milestone for me. It seemed only right that I share my thoughts with my dad, relatives, and friends – so I wrote. Letters poured out of our old mission typewriter. Eight hundred and one pages, single-spaced, once a week for six years – portraying the struggles of a post-Vatican II missionary confronting the poorest of the poor.

My friends in Saskatoon and my father received weekly letters. Dad was most faithful in replying. His little blue airmail ventures became part of Brazilian mail service. A grade three education left him with phonetic spelling (the way English should be spelled) and a subtle ability to analyze the complicated world of politics, violence, poverty, and life in general. "Never complain if you are in a warm and dry place," was how my dad saw life.

Following Brazil, it was a Canadian parish again and pastoral work at St. Philip Neri, Saskatoon. Time marched on and it was 1975. I had been ordained for 22 years when I was granted a fellowship award from the International Development Research Centre.

And that's where the contents of this book comes from, nothing more, nothing less. Fifteen years later, that sabbatical continues to affect my life, so I have added a few new thoughts to each month's letter. Also included are some photos, most taken by myself, a few taken by friends and family.

A Man of Letters is a book for my friends. It is not planned as a great piece of literature. It is a letter to those I love, and I want to do it while I still have time.

Fr. Bob Ogle

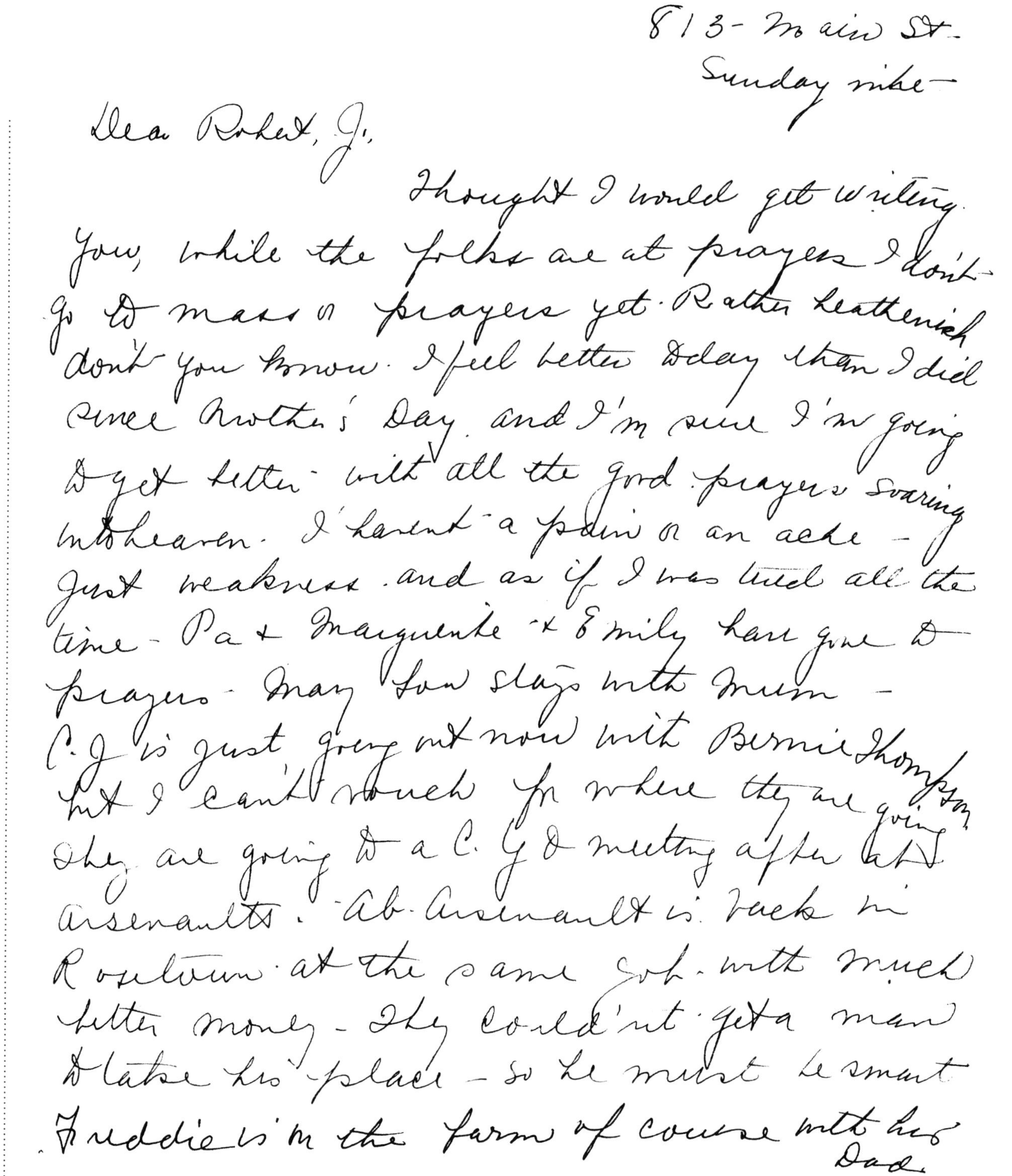
813 - Main St.
Sunday nite -

Dear Robert, Jr.,

Thought I would get writing you, while the folks are at prayers I don't go to mass or prayers yet. Father Leatherich don't you know. I feel better today than I did since Mother's Day. and I'm sure I'm going to get better - with all the good prayers soaring into heaven. I haven't a pain or an ache - just weakness and as if I was tired all the time - Pa & Marguerite & Emily have gone to prayers - Mary Lou stays with Mum - C.J. is just going out now with Bernie Thompson but I can't vouch for where they are going. They are going to a C.Y.O. meeting after at Arsenaults. Ab Arsenault is back in Rosetown at the same job - with much better money - They couldn't get a man to take his place - so he must be smart. Freddie is on the farm of course with his Dad.

Last letter of Mary Ogle to Father Bob, May 1952

On writing letters . . .

A letter has arrived, post-marked Brazil. My brother R.J. has arrived in my living room via pen, paper, and stamps.

Letter writing is an art, an art that is, regretfully, dying. Form letters spewed out in the hundreds per minute from copiers, fax machines, and word processors have pushed aside crisp writing paper and penmanship. "We regret to inform you"; "Your services will no longer be required"; "Our records show you are in arrears"; "You are invited to attend" . . . These are all phrases we are familiar with. Form letters have taken on a language of their own. They carry such strong messages and convey change . . . our letter from Rome was one such letter.

Letters, *real* letters, take discipline and thoughtful consideration. I delight in each one sent and each one received. I can't help but smile privately when I hold the carefully penned greetings from my niece's five-year-old daughter, Christina. For a few minutes she took the time to think about me, and that feels good.

Recently, Bob found the last letter our mother had written before her death in June 1952. Carefully saved (and reprinted here), I can hold this letter and remember her joy and unerring commitment to writing Bob at the seminary. Signed with love, the letters were carefully folded and placed in blue-line envelopes, addressed properly with a S.A.G. (St. Anthony Guide that Letter!) in the lower left-hand corner, stamped, and mailed. I can recall her selfless generosity, sent with those letters. I remember, also, the brief and witty letters of my father: notes of encouragement and "continued good health." When I attended nursing school as a young woman, his letters arrived without fail. Today, when it is too late to make amends for it, I live with the knowledge that his letters to me at that time often went unanswered. I was young . . . I was too busy . . . I had more important things to do . . .

Bob and I, both, have taken up this family tradition of letter-writing. It has become a central part of our daily lives. At Christmastime, over 300 hand-written notes leave my home! Bob's letters here are a tribute to that tradition and are also a timeless companion for those who would like to walk down a dusty road in Brazil, through a crowded market in India, or a struggling town in Saskatchewan.

For those of you who know Bob, or who will come to know him here, you will know of his special commitment to taking the time to communicate in written form. The letters you will read here may have been sent to a hundred people, but they spoke directly, personally to each one of us. Bob told us what was really going on in the countries he visited. His writings were not a tourist's narrative of where he had been and what he had seen; rather they were a storytelling inspired by walking with people, regardless of their faith. A cup of tea at the kitchen table, a good read, and the conversation was complete.

Mary Lou Ogle.

India

Father Bob, 1975

"It is all scarcely one long lifetime away from the buffalo herds and the camps of the Cree."

The Battleford letter was the beginning. I had no idea what would happen during the coming months. But I needed space to start—and being quiet and praying is a great way to start anything. Since then I have begun many things—politics, television, illness—and I have learned it doesn't matter how fast you run if you don't know where you are or which direction you want to go. This letter still tells me: know who you are, where you are, where you've come from, and where you are going.

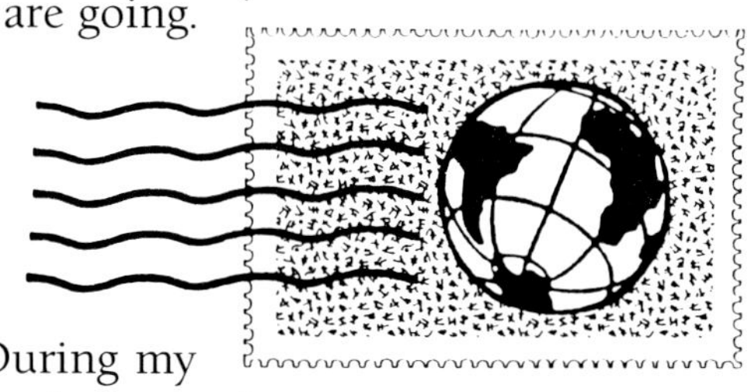

Battleford, Saskatchewan
August 1, 1975

Peace!

These ramblings will be the first of several coming your way during the next year. During my sabbatical, I hope to communicate my impressions and experiences once in a while from wherever I may be. While these messages cannot take the place of personal letters, they will at least be a contact.

During these past few days, I have been spending some time at rest and recollection here at St. Charles Scholasticate in Battleford. For those unfamiliar with the scholasticate, a word of description might be in order. It is housed in one of the historical buildings of Western Canada. It was originally built about 100 years ago as the first Government House of the North-West Territories, and the government sessions of 1878, '79, and '81 were held in it. Battleford was planned as the capital of the North-West Territories, but the Canadian Pacific Railroad spoiled all that when it passed through the southern part of the province. The capital was moved to Regina in 1883, and since that time the building has been used as an Anglican residential school for Indians, a Seventh-Day Adventist college, and the scholasticate for the Oblates of St. Mary's Province.

At this point in time, there are only a few of the oblates left here, as the scholasticate has been moved to Edmonton. Five novices and several priests and brothers run a large farm and printing press. Rooms full of dusty books, an abandoned hockey rink, a well-kept graveyard, a great cut-stone shrine to Our Lady, and other remnants of an active but nearly abandoned religious foundation remain.

The place is quiet, peaceful, and conducive to recollection and prayer. The ghosts of the Riel Rebellion are here about. From my window I can look across the tree-lined banks of the Battle River and see the reconstructed Battleford Fort. It is all scarcely one long lifetime away

St. Charles Scholasticate, Battleford, Sask.

from the buffalo herds and the camps of the Cree. Saskatchewan-born citizens have a short historical past.

Only the sounds of birds, an occasional muffled telephone ring, and the just-audible hum of traffic on the Yellowhead route break the prairie-parkland silence.

In a strange way, I felt akin to the English poet John Keats this week—or rather I should say to one of his poems. Keats did not have the opportunity to learn Greek. His contemporary poets, on the whole, seemed to have a Greek background and used Greek mythology as a source of much of their imagery. Finally it happened that somebody gave Keats a collection of the Greek classics translated by the Elizabethan writer Chapman several centuries earlier. Keats read it from cover to cover without stopping and at the end wrote one of my favourite English sonnets:

On First Looking Into Chapman's Homer

Much have I travelled in the realms of gold,
And many goodly states and kingdoms seen;
Round many western islands have I been
Which bards in fealty to Apollo hold.
Oft of one wide expanse had I been told
That deep-browed Homer ruled as his demesne;
Yet did I never breathe its pure serene
Till I heard Chapman speak out loud and bold.
Then felt I like some watcher of the skies
When a new planet swims into his ken;
Or like stout Cortez when with eagle eyes
He stared at the Pacific—and all his men
Looked at each other with a wild surmise—
Silent, upon a peak in Darien.

I had set myself to peruse the Gospel of St. Matthew and as many of the Vatican Council II documents as I could review. In doing so, it was almost like doing something new again. It had been some years since I had read the documents in chronological order. It had completely slipped my mind that the Council Fathers had issued a Statement to the Whole World at the request of Pope John XXIII only nine days after the Vatican Council had opened. It is short, but it seems to have caught the spirit of what the Council would do. It was kind of like Cortez (actually it was Balboa) catching his first sight of the Pacific after crossing the Isthmus of Panama. The statement read:

> . . . In this assembly, under the guidance of the Holy Spirit, we wish to inquire how we ought to renew ourselves, so that we may be found increasingly faithful to the Gospel of Christ. We shall take pains so to present to men of this age God's truth in its integrity and purity that they may understand it and gladly assent to it.

> . . . Coming together in unity from every nation under the sun, we carry in our hearts the hardships, the bodily and mental distress, the sorrows, longings, and hopes of all the peoples entrusted to us. We urgently turn our thoughts to all the anxieties by which modern man is afflicted. Hence, let our concern swiftly focus first of all on those who are especially lowly, poor, and weak. Like Christ, we would have pity on the multitude weighted down with hunger, misery, and lack of knowledge. We want to fix a steady gaze on those who still lack the opportune help to achieve a way of life worthy of human beings . . .

The Council Fathers then repeated parts of a radio message of John XXIII given the previous month of September 1962. The Pope had pleaded for peace among nations and for universal social justice. The bishops ended by saying, "Our prayer is that in the midst of this world there may radiate the light of our hope in Jesus Christ, our only Saviour."

After reading this statement, I could not but feel again that optimistic and joyful mood that marked the *John* days (both Roncalli and Kennedy). The Church and church people were coming to terms with the world and with the future. Since that time, I think, other moods have set in and many struggles have been fought by people, both within themselves and in society at large.

Personally, I was bothered by the fact that I had spent so much time on "church" things that were not concerned with "the lowly, the poor, and the weak." There were so many times that I had not carried in my heart, "the hardships, the bodily and mental distress, the sorrows, longings, and hopes of all the peoples."

But it still remains clear that there is a plan there, although one needing a great deal of updating if another Council were to be called. It is already "historical." One morning this week I had coffee with the novices and I found out that these young men, on the whole, could not remember pre-Vatican II times! *Somebody* is getting old.

On the 22nd of August, I will be leaving Saskatoon and going to London and Rome with a Pilgrimage Group which we are calling the "Saskatchewan People." There are members from the dioceses of Prince Albert, Saskatoon, and Gravelbourg. When they return to Canada, I will remain in Paris for 10 weeks of intensive French before coming back to Ottawa to begin a program of research and study in international development. So it's back to the books until we meet again.

Au revoir,

Roberto

P.S. An old retired priest told me this week, "Religion means to believe in God and be willing to take the consequences."

St. Peter's, Rome

"You can hear the patter of centuries of sandals in the corridors."

I have been to Rome many times since this letter. I remain fascinated with the Eternal City and have encountered political skills there that I was never able to understand. I still don't know when "yes" means "no." I prefer to look at it as St. Matthew did: "All you need to say is 'yes' if you mean 'yes' and 'no' if you mean 'no.'" (Matthew, 5,37). Life has become much simpler for me since my days of tension with Rome. Serious illness cleans the slate of trivial but crushing stresses. Now I believe that every human being has only three things to do: to live, to suffer, and to die. It is a universal call shared by all. It was a trail blazed by Jesus. Most people fear death, almost all of us fear suffering, and a great many fear life, the kind of life that sets them free.

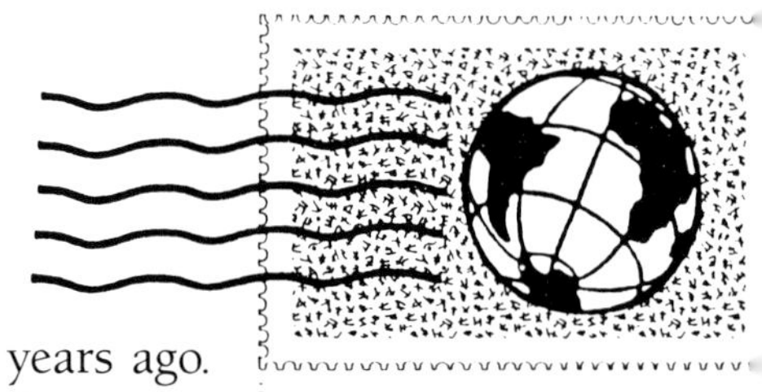

Roma
September 1, 1975

Peace!

This week we are living on the exact spot where the Roman emperors lived 2,000 years ago. We are right in the heart of ancient Rome; tourists come here by the millions each year to gaze at the ruins of the Roman Forum and the Palatine Hills. We can do the same by opening our window. Immediate suspicion would suggest that we must be bedded down in a Hilton, because one knows that only Hilton or the Sons of St. Francis would be able to own such a site . . .

Hotel Casa Kolbe is an old Franciscan monastery converted into a modern-day hostel for Roman pilgrims. It has retained its ancient space, wide corridors, chapel, and cloister garden. The ancient building has been redone and provides large, simple, but comfortable rooms with individual Italian-marble bathrooms. The refectory provides basic but most-adequate meals. The Franciscans still live here on the top floor, and if you listen hard at night, you can hear the patter of centuries of sandals in the corridors.

The hotel takes its name from the Franciscan priest, Blessed Maximilia Kolbe, who gave his life in the Nazi death-camp of Auschwitz so that another man might live. This business of "giving one's life that another might live" has a terrible Christian ring about it, and Rome is full of the markers that point to those who found this possible.

At this time, we make up part of an English group that came down from London last Sunday "by charter." It is something like the Second Battalion of the Regina Rifles joining the Royal Fusiliers on the line at Passchendaele in 1916.

If I were a good storyteller, I would regularly take charter flights and find out how and

St. Peter's from the Oblate Scholasticate, Rome

why 180 ragamuffin people come together on a certain day at a certain airport and fly to a certain place for a certain time. Such a story of people booking off 20 days from their lives would be interesting indeed. (Chaucer had stumbled on the same idea some time ago . . .)

Today we went to the English College along with our English co-pilgrims for "tea and penitential service." The gory paintings on the chapel walls depict the 44 former alumni who took the hard way out in Elizabethan times. The college had first been opened in 1350 to house English pilgrims coming for the second Holy Year. Our guide explained that it became the college to train priests at the time of Henry VIII, "when this business got rather messy in England." The guide, an English seminarian, had a fabulous sense of dry humour. Among other things, he remarked on the hole in the priceless painting on the refectory wall, some 15 feet above the door. (The painting depicts Mary Magdalene washing the feet of our Lord, "while the Apostles were in a flap about the price of balm or some such thing.") The hole had been made when one of their seminarians had thrown an apple at another colleague who had been skipping out the door at the time. That was one seminarian, it seems, who could never have made the British cricket team!

Since 1300, the Church has set aside four years each century for special prayer and reflection on where she is going, and where the world is going. These Jubilee Years are a time to "re-establish peace, between ourselves and God; a time of reconciliation," Pope Paul said last Christmas. They have always been marked with people coming to pray at the tombs of the Apostles.

* * * * * * * *

The exodus of the "Saskatchewan People" from the all-too-inadequate Saskatoon airport was something not unlike survivors leaving a city about to fall to enemy attack. However, the send-off we received from the Ursulines at Glengarda, Saskatoon, with a special lunch, liturgy, and sing-song, made the inconveniences of the airport departure easy to forget.

Every time that I am in a fully loaded plane with fuel, passengers, luggage, and sagging wings, I wonder if the runway will be long enough to prove the principle once more that a flat surface propelled with enough force against a block of air will rise–but rise she did, and our Boeing 707, brimming with people, swung over Sutherland to wend its way through a line of thunderstorms and finally catch the polar route that would take us into Gatwick Airport, London, in just over eight hours. As the Canada we knew fell away beneath the fleecy stratus of tundra-covering clouds, and the confident British voice of the pilot assured us that we were high above Greenland, a full moon rising over the Arctic was reflecting in shining silver on the right wing, at the same time as the remnants of the setting summer sun kept the left wing ablaze in golden flaming glory.

In Britain, the "Saskatchewan People" had a chance to find out why mounties wear red coats, why we vote for members of Parliament, why there is a system known as jury trial, and why we generally speak English–all these traditions have their roots in England. A tour of Windsor Castle, a visit to Shakespeare's home, a play at the Royal Haymarket Theatre brought an understanding of our country that living in Prince Albert could never bring.

We joined in with the thousands or hundreds of thousands who are flocking from continental Europe because it is cheaper to holiday in England. The White Cliffs of Dover and the British sterling have proven formidable barriers to all invaders for centuries. The White Cliffs are still there and prove no less formidable, but the sterling has withered before a 28 per cent inflationary spiral. Many who would have hesitated before are now pouring in from Germany, Holland, France, Israel, Denmark, Spain, Rumania . . . you name it. And be quite sure that scarcely a person will understand you from Piccadilly to Trafalgar Square. English is the last language you hear.

For me, a highlight of our English sojourn was a visit to the church at Stoke Poges, which has remained untarnished though millions have come to see the place where Thomas Gray wrote one of the most famous of all English poems: "Elegy Written in a Country Church-yard." The same yew tree he sat under to pen those famous lines is still there, and the overall truth of what he wrote still holds today:

> Let not ambition mock their useful toil,
> Their homely joys, and destiny obscure;
> Nor grandeur hear with a disdainful smile
> The short and simple annals of the poor.
>
> The boast of heraldry, the pomp of pow'r,
> And all that beauty, all that wealth e'er gave,
> Await alike th' inevitable hour:
> The paths of glory lead but to the grave.

Catholic life in England is also different from what I have known in Canada. A Faith that has been cradled in 400 years of minority existence, that has been nurtured with the names of those who died at Tyburn Hill to be faithful to Rome and the ancient creeds does not easily adopt the customs and practices that a 20th-century Council might think to bring about.

We attended Mass at Westminster Cathedral–a great mass of brickwork and helter-skelter marble and plaques–built in the early 20th century as a *sign* of the living return of the Catholic Faith to England. The cathedral is being rapidly obscured by a beehive of glass-faced, module-type, "clockwork orange" office buildings that are sprouting up around Victoria Station. The Mass was in Latin, celebrated by a priest with his back toward the people and swathed in reams of incense, as a feeble choir sang Mass VIII and Credo III. The introduction to the little Latin

Mass book, "Jubilate Deo," that the people were using, explained that "provision should be made, however, to see that the faithful can also say or sing together in Latin those parts of the Ordinary of the Mass that concern them." (Vatican Council II, Constitution on Sacred Liturgy, no. 54.) The readings, however, were in flawless BBC English, and the sermon was a most scholarly explanation of the "Rock and Peter" passage that remained as mysterious and as far away from the people as the rest of the celebration.

Over the summer as we had prepared for "a return to our religious, cultural, and linguistic roots," I became aware that the name we had given ourselves, the "Saskatchewan People," and which we used on our green-and-gold name tags, really did say who we were. With people whose origins were in Bellevue, Creighton (near Lac Pelletier), Shell Lake, Moose Jaw, Krydor, Birch Hills, Prelate, Wisconsin, St. John's, Russia, Ireland, and Rosetown; and with accents that were quite distinguishably French, German, Irish, Ukrainian, American, Newfie, and Saskatchewan, there could be no doubt that we were well named.

Here in Rome, we are to see the Pope tomorrow and go to Assisi on Thursday. A few days later, the "Saskatchewan People" will wing their way up over Iceland once more for Saskatoon. I will go to Paris and begin a new "French Revolution" at the Alliance Française.

Until the next time: ARRIVEDERCI!

Roberta

"... the new universal language that has replaced Latin – the visual simple prayer drawn by children and understood by all mankind."

My days in Paris were happy ones. I seriously tried to learn French. It should have been easy. My mother and father were bilingual but spoke French at home only when they did not want the children to know what was happening. Many more hours of French classes when I was an M.P., and living in a French community should have done the trick. But I have remained crippled as a unilingual in Canada. My advice to young people is to learn as many languages as they can, for each language will open a new door on the world.

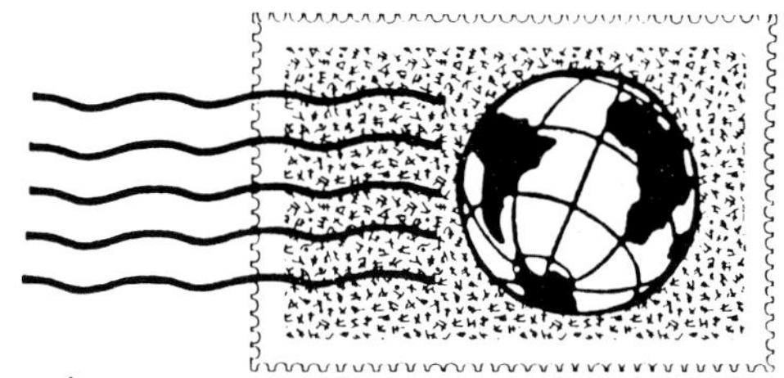

170 Bd. du Montparnasse
75014, Paris, France
October 1, 1975

PAIX!

Autumn in Paris is soft, like a gentle Indian summer. At times it rains, and sometimes it even rains hard, but when the clouds pass away and the sun comes out . . . soft is the only way to describe it.

The long avenues of well-kept trees, the brown leaves of the chestnuts wafting to the cobblestones, the strollers, the flower shops, the sidewalk cafés, the children hurrying with their school books and long loaves of French bread – all blend together with the smells of strong tobacco, exquisite perfumes, diesel smoke, and autumn. It is Paris in the fall.

The Redemptorist residence where I am staying appears from the outside to be an apartment block not unlike countless others lining the streets and boulevards. However, when one enters through the glass doors that open off the Boulevard de Montparnasse, you find yourself immediately in the confines of a friendly home. This is the provincial house of the French Redemptorists, but they have made it into a hostel for priests and other students. At the back there is a beautiful little garden marred only by the sound of harsh bells from a girls' school a short distance away in the old St. Vincent de Paul Hospital.

Three minutes down the street is one of the largest parks in Paris, the Luxembourg Gardens, which surround the French Senate. The palace that houses the Senate was built by Marie de Medici, wife of Henry IV, to remind her of her home in central Italy. The palace was finished in 1630, but Cardinal Richelieu saw fit to have her banished to Cologne where she died in 1642. I doubt if any of the thousands who pass their afternoons in the park could care less. Old men in crumpled suits playing checkers or feeding the birds, young lovers aware of nothing except themselves, mothers pushing their baby carriages, grandmothers showing each other snapshots of their grandchildren, students doing their homework, little boys sailing their boats in the basins surrounding the statues and fountains . . . everybody soaking up the September sun and enjoying the trees, the flowers, the quiet, and the ice cream sold by street vendors. Paris is more than a city; it is a way of life.

But the face of Paris is changing. At one time I could have said, Paris is five storeys tall, and not been very wrong. Now, however, the skyline is being broken by new skyscrapers—modern towers of steel and glass that push their way up over the historic sites. One can see hundreds of building cranes (from the top of our home here); the long counterweighted booms that turn right, turn left, lift up, let down, and look all the world like a flock of giant flamingoes having breakfast in a shallow lake shore in East Africa.

My room at "170" is small but adequate. People are here from all over the world: returned missionaries, doctoral students, administrators, visitors. The meals are excellent and very French. Spanish Sisters look after the house. The dress is completely nonclerical. There are three concelebrated Masses each day—times are arranged to fit the different schedules. The liturgies are prayerful, and except for the albed main celebrant, devoid of liturgical vestments. *The language is French and for that reason I am here.*

On September 15th, I started at the Alliance Française. It was the opening day of school in Paris, and on the 10-minute walk to class I felt very much a part of the children we met, who were being taken by their mothers, with books and lunch in hand, to start their first day of school. They were four, and I was 46, and my "mother" was a priest from Bombay who had started French two weeks before. Like the four-year-olds, I envied the blue-jeaned teenagers hanging around the floor of a "Lycée," smoking cigarettes, and looking as though they knew the answers to everything.

The Alliance Française was founded in 1883 to promote the French language and culture. Students attend it from all over the world. My first day in class: a Japanese in front of me, a Pole to my right, a Nigerian behind me, and a Costa Rican to my left. I maneuvered through various classes until at last I found my *level.* The building is old; the marble stairways have deep troughs near the corner post at each landing, where millions of shoes have worn away the stone as they made the turn to go up the next flight. The rooms are dark and dirty, and the benches are long, uncomfortable, scratched, carved, and marked. The washrooms—shared by men and women—have graffiti written in 30 languages. The lighting is poor . . . *but* the instruction is excellent! The teachers are "pros"; their techniques and systems are the best that I have seen. If I do not learn a great deal of French, I will at least have studied under the best. It is like learning to drive from Fitipaldi or one of the other Formula I drivers on the Grand

Prix . . . much better than trying to learn French by translating the ads on the back of a box of corn flakes.

We have four hours of intensive instruction from 8:30 until 12:30 each day, and I do about four hours of homework at home. At the end of the day, *je suis tres fatigué*. On weekends I spend part of Saturday seeing the sights and sounds of Paris, and then work on a little plan to be in a different parish each Sunday to see how things are done here, church-wise. I have already seen enough to keep me going for a good number of years when I return to Canada.

I arrived in Paris on a Sunday, after a terrible crossing by night-ferry from Southampton, England. The taxi driver who drove me from the train station to the dockside explained, "Jerry used to fly down 'ere and 'it everything in sight . . . didn't get that church though [a huge Norman structure], t'weren't on the main road, ye'see. Couldn't go after 'im myself as much as I would 'ave liked to . . . born with this bum leg . . . drove a taxi then too, but 'e never broke my spirit, Jerry didn't, just made me mad." Really quite an interesting monologue on the 35th anniversary of the Battle of Britain victory.

My seasickness was still with me when I arrived in Paris, but a few hours of rest and some crackers and Vichy water made it possible to go out to the 5:30 Mass in Notre-Dame-des-Champs, the local parish. There was a regular hodgepodge collection of late-afternoon worshippers, but the celebrant did a beautiful job of bringing the people into the spirit of a worshipping community. At the sign of peace, a middle-aged lady turned around and kissed me right cheek, left cheek, right cheek. I felt that I had won the Croix de Guerre.

I found something beautiful on the walls, too – the drawings and art work of little children. It could have been in St. Philip's. There was no way of telling that they were drawn by little Parisians; just gloriously coloured mums and dads, dogs and cats, birds and trees. To me it said: Here is the new universal language that has replaced Latin – the visual, simple prayer drawn by children and understood by all mankind.

Au revoir,

Roberto

P.S. When I arrived, I had about 25 letters waiting from five continents. *Quelle richesse!*

Vimy Ridge, France

Engraved in Vimy Memorial

"'Thou shalt not kill,' the Lord said."

I have returned to Vimy many times. It always leaves me with the haunting question of what good and evil are all about. A landmark to the birth of Canadian nationhood, the endless graveyards leave me with a hollow feeling. There had to be a better way. I have visited Vimy with my father, with my sister Mary Lou, with parliamentary delegations, and with my youngest niece, Katherine Kebe. Everyone responds differently. But the single name of "Ogle" on the monument, among the names of thousands who have no known burial place, tells me that my history is ground into the mud of Flanders. I know for sure that I have never fired a bullet at another human being, and I have never had anyone fire at me. I thank God that I was born in my time and place. Countless others have not been so lucky. Sometimes, it comes down to the luck of the draw.

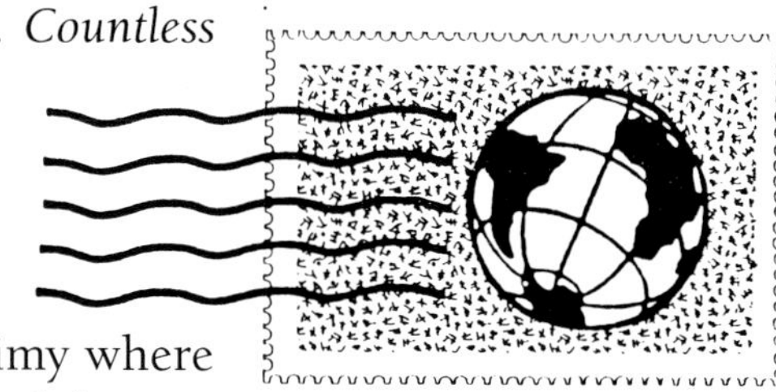

Vimy Ridge
November 1, 1975

Today is All Saints, a holyday and holiday in France; I drove with some friends to Vimy where a high, steep ridge runs across the plains of Flanders. At the top, on ground deeded forever to Canada by the French people, is a huge monument bearing this inscription: *The Canadian Corps on the 9th of April, 1917, with four divisions in line on a front of four miles attacked and captured this ridge.*

More Canadians died violent deaths that day than on any other day in history. Some say that was how Canada became a nation, but that would be open to argument.

A truly unearthly quiet hung over the empty trenches, the shell-torn land, and the neat cemeteries. The hill was muddy from the cold fall rain, and it was too late in the year for poppies. The smell of wet autumn leaves and thick grass filled the air. In the end I knew there would only be the grass. All else passes. Nobody would remember what the "Guns of August" were all about.

We began the month of All Souls with the trip to Vimy. We came back through Douai and Reims, a one-time journey to piece together the enigma of life, death, suffering, violence, glory, time, and eternity; for in due course, all must come to the eleventh hour of the eleventh day of the eleventh month.

I sent my last letter out from Paris a few days before the October 1st deadline, hoping that nothing important would happen before it "went to press." However, such was not the case. The last week of September in Paris was very interesting indeed. On the day that the five urban guerillas were shot in Spain, huge anti-Franco demonstrations were organized on the Champs-Élysées. This is a type of political activity that a prairie boy doesn't run into every day. The exact number of participants would only be a guess, but it was a Saturday, and the weather was good . . . let's just leave it at four times the population of the Hub City.

Three things impressed me about the demonstrations. First, the violence with which the demonstrators demonstrated against violence. (They broke all the windows in the street, and burned the cars that happened to be parked there.) Second, the skill, if you could call it that, which the police had in breaking up the demonstration . . . they really play for keeps. Third, I thought it was rather a strange thing to see so many Frenchmen demonstrating against violence when they were running right over the places where the swish-chop of the guillotine had been a common sound.

During the demonstrations, I kept my distance and wore my running shoes. I didn't want to get knocked down by a club-swinging gendarme . . .

Violence is certainly one of the most ambiguous realities that we have in our midst today. It goes from the spanking Johnnie gets for raiding the cookie jar, through the widespread starvation imposed on peoples by unjust economic and political systems, to the electronically aimed and controlled B–52 saturation bombings of Vietnam. Real violence has been experienced by very few of us who have Western Canadian roots. No enemy tanks have ever rolled down Number 7 Highway; 2nd Avenue has never been devastated by an air raid; Gunworth was never picked as the site for an extermination camp; no government has been overturned by armed uprising or a headsman's axe; no family wiped out because induced starvation was brought to bear against it. These are realities that are a long way away from most of us . . . but they are, and have been, part and parcel of most of the world's history.

One of the principal *monuments* of Paris is the Hotel des Invalides . . . It houses the tomb of Napoleon, as well as one of the largest military museums in the world. Within it there is a sample or model of nearly everything from the stone that Cain used to kill Abel to the most modern weaponry devised by humans to maim or destroy each other . . . bludgeons, spears, lances, swords, cutlasses, daggers, bayonets, maces, axes, pikes, flintlocks, pistols, muskets, revolvers, cannons, mortars, missiles, bullets, grenades, mines, arrows, crossbows, flame-throwers, breach loaders, self-loaders, tanks, armoured cars, rocket launchers, galleys, cruisers, submarines, corvettes, battleships, poison gas, bombs, shrapnel . . . to name a few. Tradenames: Mauser, Springfield, Webley, Rolls Royce, Boeing, Mitsubishi, Peugeot, Fokker, Colt, Messerschmitt, Browning, General Motors, Lee-Enfield, Daussault, Krupp, etc.

Each generation found a different way to dress the participants, and the uniforms of the young French recruits who were visiting the museum while I was there looked very drab compared to their counterparts of former times.

I suppose what impressed me the most about the whole thing, though, were two little seven-year-old boys who had defied the sign of "NE TOUCHEZ PAS" and were mowing down the imaginary enemy with a captured World War I machine gun.

And so what does it all say? It would seem that some of the world is coming to a new kind of consciousness or understanding about violence. The fact that so many people protested against the five executions would have been an impossible thought 30 years ago. Furthermore, I would say that there is a new realization of the political power of well-planned, small-scale, urban, guerilla action and its ability to force diplomatic bargaining which a full-scale war could not.

But there are still so many unanswered moral questions. "Thou shalt not kill," the Lord said. Of all the commandments, that one has received the most padding of "ifs," "whens," and "buts." Yet, haunting suppositions remain. If it had not been for the French Revolution, would the Bourbons still be at Versailles? Without the violence, we might have a Louis XXIV, and of course, Dickens would never have written, *A Tale of Two Cities*.

At the Alliance Française, the "Bataille de 70 Jours" is coming to an end. It has been a good experience. Some days, when the imperfect tense was being mixed up with the conditional, I took heart from a marble plaque inside the main door. It lists the names of all the presidents of the Alliance since 1883 and the years they acted in that capacity. Some of the great men of French letters have their names there. The last one on the list is Wilfred Baumgartner, 1966. On bad days, I tell myself that he must have been some guy who came along to take a 10-week crash course and stayed to take the place over. There are thousands of alumni all over the world. Some years back, a student by the name of J. B. Montini got his start in French here . . . He still has an Italian accent though . . . Our teacher has kept the same high quality of excellence, although sometimes she reminds me a little bit of Madame Defarge.

I saw the movie "Rollerball" in English with French subtitles. The French people missed a lot in the translation. The movie is a violent parable that says to me: Capitalism is like a game of rollerball.

I do not know when these thoughts will reach you. Another kind of violence, I suppose, will decide when that happens. The mail strike in Canada has affected many people who know nothing about it. In the French post offices, there are two signs over the mail slots. The first says that normal mail contact has been resumed with Saigon and South Vietnam. The second says that there is no mail service in Canada. Besides missing news from home, the embarrassing questions posed by many classmates of "What's wrong with Canada?" were hard to answer. Maybe some of you know!

Au revoir!

Roberto

Henry B. Ogle and Sunnyside homestead, Sask.

"The only thing I know for sure about this historic place is that there is No River and there is No Bar."

Like many other small pioneer towns, Rivière Qui Barre is fading. It has been a part of my history because it was a part of my father's history. Mary Fitzgerald, my stepmother, called it home. Now her body lies buried in the little churchyard. I celebrated the liturgy of her passing on March 17, 1982, because her brother, Father Walter Fitzgerald, had been too ill to officiate that day.

All across Western Canada, small towns are dying. The pressures of debt, big business, falling prices, and international markets are driving people away. Around the world, similar conditions are forcing people to leave the rural areas and move to cities like São Paulo, Cairo, or Calcutta. A slum in a sprawling city is anything but a pleasant and healthy place to live.

In 1989, I took an old friend, Matt Dales, to visit his native town of McGee, Saskatchewan. He had not been home for nearly 50 years. For all intents and purposes, McGee has disappeared. Everything, including the elevators, the train station, the stores, the homes, and the school, had vanished. Only an eerie silence and the feeling of touching a corpse remained.

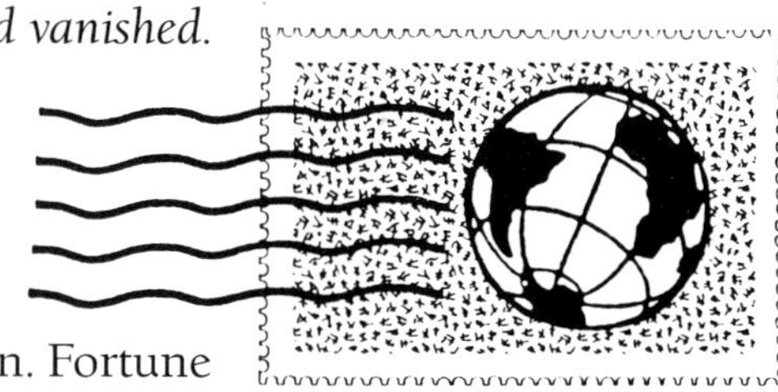

Rivière Qui Barre, Alberta
December 1, 1975

In the late 1890s, gold was discovered in the Klondike. By 1898, the famous Rush was on. Fortune seekers from the whole world converged on one of the most hidden places on the globe, where Robert Service asked those who did not go, if they had ever "gazed on naked grandeur, where there's nothing else to gaze on . . . " Sam McGee, Dangerous Dan McGrew, and the Lady that was known as Lou became part of our folklore.

There were two main routes into the gold fields. One route took would-be miners up the Pacific coast and in over the Chilkoot Pass. The other became known as the "Back-door Route" or "The All-Canadian Route." The latter began in the frontier town of Edmonton and wended its way over the whitened bones of those who had gone ahead. Its main disadvantage, outside of the fact that very few managed to live through its ordeals, was that the gold seekers arrived two years after the rush was over . . . the beginning, I suppose, of many other "All-Canadian" adventures.

One of the first stopovers on the trail was a booming little town with hotels, outfitters, blacksmith shops, and saloons, that was known as Rivière Qui Barre. It had begun when settlers broke the fertile land some 20 miles northwest of Father Lacombe's base Mission of St. Albert. Bishop Grandin had visited it in 1895 and decided to have a church built there. Later, tales of diabolical possession, exorcisms, ghosts, etc., added to the town's character. The railroad missed it. No grain elevators were ever built. The hotels, stores, and outfitters disappeared, as would have the town if a large centralized school had not been built there in the recent past. The village is of special interest to me because my dad has been retired there for the last 15 years. He makes up a hefty percentage of the population, which hovers around 30 souls. The only thing I know for sure about this historic place is that there is No River and there is No Bar.

Paris is now a memory . . . The 10 weeks went very quickly. In all, there were 47 days of instruction at the Alliance Française. I did not become bilingual in any sense of the word, but I did pick up a surprising amount . . . surprising, at least for me, because language is not my *forte*. As a basic preparation for social action work, I could think of nothing better than language learning. It is a situation in which one is always wrong, and I think the real virtue of the great social changers has been the ability and the patience to live with the frustration of always seeing the reality and the possibility of change differently from the majority of people . . . *to be always wrong.*

Of course, Paris had a lot more than the Alliance Française. Many famous people have lived around the district where I stayed . . . Lenin and Trotsky did their waiting in this *quartier*. Picasso and Einstein had rooms nearby. The Closerie des Lilas Café across the street was where Hemingway and his crowd hung out in the 1920s. In front of that café is a statue of Maréchal Ney, Napoleon's general, Prince of Moscow. Cast in bronze and well tinted by passing pigeons, it has the Maréchal triumphantly advancing over the fallen enemy. On each side of the base are long lists of battle names and dates. The last is Waterloo, 1815. Napoleon got St. Helena; Ney faced a firing squad where the statue now stands—a kind of pre-Nuremberg war crimes justice . . . great losers!

About eight blocks behind the Redemptorist house is the laboratory of Louis Pasteur. Louis probably did more to change the history of the world than any other person in the last 100 years. He found out that boiling water would kill germs. In a generation, European populations exploded; immigrations and migrations to the New World became imperative. Life spans, family sizes, traditional morality, housing, transportation, food—all were rocked as they had never been rocked before. I wonder who will be the next person to pull a "Louis."

For those who like trivia, I think the following is interesting. The French National Observatory is about 225 yards east of the room where I stayed. The latitude of the observatory is 48 degrees, 50 minutes, 11 seconds north of the equator. If someone went to the Saskatchewan-Montana border, and drove straight east for about 6,000 miles, he would end up in the northern suburbs of Paris. That's one piece of trivia. The other is that the observatory was the Paris Meridian from 1667 on. It was the starting point for those explorers who sailed west and wanted to know how far they had gone. It remained the Meridian until 1884 (probably longer if Waterloo had gone the other way) when Greenwich, England, became the centre of the world for navigation and time measurement. All the countries in the world accepted the Greenwich Meridian, except France and Ireland, who hung onto the Paris Meridian until 1911 . . . which goes to show that no real Irishman would be caught using an English meridian. So much for trivia.

As of this week, I will begin my year of research with the International Development Research Centre in Ottawa. The I.D.R.C. is a public corporation established by an act of Parliament in 1970.

The objectives of the Centre are to initiate, encourage, support, and conduct research into the problems of the developing regions of the world and into the means for applying and adapting scientific, technical, and other knowledge to the economic and social advancement of those regions, and, in carrying out those objectives:

a) to enlist the talents of natural and social scientists and technologists of Canada and other countries
b) to assist the developing regions to build up the research capabilities, the innovative skills, and the institutions required to solve their problems
c) to encourage generally the coordination of international development research
d) to foster cooperation in research on development issues between the developed and developing regions for their mutual benefit

Each year, 10 Canadians are picked for particular studies. All must be middle-aged and have 10 years of professional experience in some field. The Research Associate Award is designed to "provide opportunities for Canadian professionals at the mid-career level to take a 'Sabbatical Year' to undertake training, research, or investigation in the international development field."

My particular research will be to "study the real lasting effects of projects in developing countries funded by Canadian Volunteer Agencies . . . in particular, the Canadian Catholic Organization for Development and Peace."

My real hope is that I will be able to observe, study, and research the possibilities of finding a workable pastoral to make the Constitution–"The Church in the Modern World"– more of a reality in the lives of individuals, parishes, dioceses, and countries.

During the year, I will be in and out of the country as the program progresses. At this time I do hope that each and every one of you have a Holy and Happy Christmas and a great 1976. The Gospel antiphon for Advent is to the point. "Lord let us see your kindness, and grant us your Salvation."

Roberto

"... it's too bad that today's poor have to sell their souls to either the Hard Political Right or the Hard Political Left."

When I visited Cuba for New Year's 1976, I went as a tourist. But I have been back to Cuba as an international parliamentarian. When I met Fidel Castro, I poked him in the chest, (a Latin American gesture of friendship) and asked him, "How is it that you went to a Jesuit high school and turned out to be a communist?" He never blinked, rubbed his nose as he does when he's serious, and said, "The Jesuits taught me two things. They taught me morality and they taught me discipline." If I were to write a book on Cuba, I would call it Morality and Discipline. Everybody eats, has a dwelling, goes to school, and has medical attention; but it is dull—just like Jesuit high school.

Today's changes in Eastern Europe and Central America leave Castro's Cuba in a unique position. How much longer it can defy the winds of change is anybody's guess.

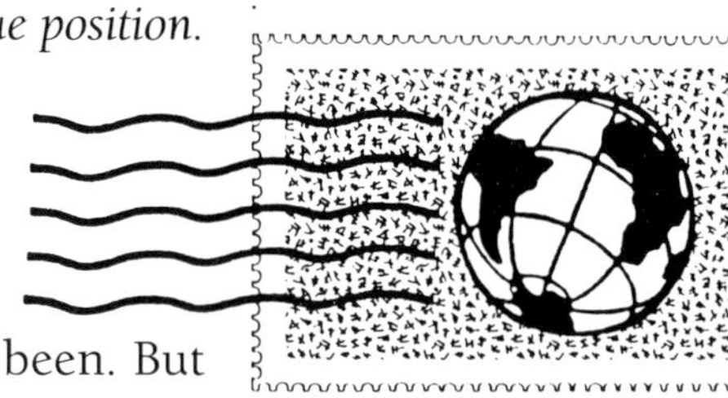

Varadero, Cuba
January 1, 1976

Christopher Columbus found Cuba in 1492. It was in the same place it had always been. But he and his crew thought they were in India, which is why they called the natives, "Indians."

Havana was established in 1514. It was to become the centre of the Spanish Main—the "jewel in the Spanish Crown." In 40 years, the 100,000 or so original Cubans were wiped out by the Christian conquerors. Countless African slaves were brought in to labour on the new sugar and tobacco plantations.

After over four centuries with Indians, conquistadors, slaves, pirates, revolutionaries, Teddy Roosevelt's Roughriders, sugar barons, and mafia, Fidel Castro and 80 bearded companions took power 17 years ago today. Since then he has threaded a thin line of existence between the forces of East and West.

Through the officially guarded, guided, superficial eyes of a Canadian tourist on an air-conditioned, ultramodern, Spanish-built bus, Cuba looks like a 760-mile slice of northeast Brazil shoved out into the Gulf Stream. The architecture, the clothing, and the climate look and feel the same. Instead of "futeball" fields, there are baseball diamonds. Canadian Holsteins mingle with local scrub cattle. Miracle mechanics keep the pre-1959 cars rolling, but tired tires slow the sparse traffic. Billboards and radio announcements with revolutionary political propaganda replace our familiar hard sell for shaving cream and Gulf Oil.

A quiet dullness reigns . . . a Third World country with a *New Five-Year Plan*. An observer

Father Bob meets Fidel Castro

must be careful to make his comparisons with northeast Brazil rather than with southern Ontario. To someone from southern Ontario, the country looks very backward. Compared to northeast Brazil, however, Cuba is very advanced. Nevertheless, it's too bad that today's poor have to sell their souls to either the Hard Political Right or the Hard Political Left.

My trip to Cuba was a few days of New Year change. In December, I had visited the headquarters of different Canadian Church denominations and agencies that fund projects in the developing world. Over 80 of these agencies have their headquarters in the "Bermuda Triangle" of Toronto, Montreal, and Ottawa. Most have closed their offices for the Christmas-New Year holiday. An official directory lists 91 groups doing this kind of work, although I think that there are actually more. I have picked 24 of them to visit because they do work in either Brazil or India, have been working for more than five years, and have a budget of around $100,000 or more. My main purpose is to visit various projects funded more than five years ago, and try to gauge what the long-term effects have been.

It meant many telephone calls, subways, secretaries, waiting rooms, buses, sloshy streets, talk, coffee, points of view, notes, literature, parking lots, Christmas parties, projects, doubts, fears, hopes, biases. I am feeling something akin to culture shock. In reality, it may be a version of future shock.

Many of the things, places, and people of Toronto were no longer as I remembered them. Everything had changed and continued to change as I trudged past. For instance, take stodgy, old, Anglo-Saxon, Protestant, Victorian Yonge Street in Toronto. Many the time I had clanged down its deserted bleakness on a Sunday-afternoon streetcar. Yonge Street, as I knew it, was gone. Same geography; different world! In its place was an international, multilingual, multicultural, constantly changing thoroughfare with everything on sale from human flesh in any colour to meals, music, art, and entertainment from any country. It is only a symptom of the far more basic life-style change that has taken place at that end of Lake Ontario.

In the 20-minute, high-speed, polluted spin across 401 from Scarborough to the airport, I could see the homes of more people than live in Saskatchewan. Forests of apartment blocks made me wonder who had sold all the electric kettles, the hair dryers, the colour televisions, the bricks, the magazines, and the liquor cabinets that made these modern, cliff-hanging, isolated caves available to those who had the keys to their locked doors.

Knowing the symptoms of culture shock from past experience, I appreciated that my observations were probably out of proportion, biased, false, angry, and frustrated. The tensions that I experienced as a Saskatchewan "immigrant" would be akin to those of an Asian, African, or Latin American. I realized that more decisions affecting my life were made in the steel-and-glass financial empires of old Yorktown, Ontario, than in the legislative buildings in Regina.

By coincidence, my studies began with the Season of Advent. This traditional time of preparation for Christmas was markedly different for me this year. In a sense, I lived a secular Advent. In every place I was meeting people who had fears and doubts about the future, loneliness, pain . . . the qualities that marked the pre-Christian waiting period through the long Jewish history. The carpenter from Nazareth and his wife knew pain and loneliness as they plodded toward Bethlehem. My own particular problem was to know whether there would be any Christ-Mass for today's people and how it would become real for them.

January 1st marks the first day of the last quarter of the 20th century. To the football "buff" this means that the game will be over in 2000. There won't be many of us around for overtime, although without a doubt another century game will go on. Some who receive these jottings can remember the opening kickoff in 1900. Orville and Wilbur Wright were still making bicycles and watching the birds. At the end of the first quarter, the old structures that made up the 19th-century game had been annihilated on the Eastern and Western fronts. Lindbergh was flying a mail plane and dreaming of the "Spirit of St. Louis." I made it into the game before halftime in 1950. Another world war had taken place and the atom had been smashed. The third quarter was dogged by "little" wars. Neil Armstrong stepped out on the moon. As the fourth quarter begins there is widespread scepticism that the British-French Concorde is too expensive, too fast, too noisy, too polluting. Is it really a final limit to growth?

I feel an apprehension on the bench by many of the players who will finish the 20th-century game. Even though the band may be playing "Let Us Reach for the Stars," most of the team is saying, "Can We Hold the Line?"

A Christmas card I received had the following wish that I pass along to you. "At this holy time, may we find love where there is hate, faith where there is doubt, hope where there is despair, light where there is darkness, joy where there is sadness, and peace where there is strife."

Abraços,

Roberto

". . . if we have no love for the people, it is all in vain."

Ottawa is one of my favourite cities. It was here, in 1976, that I had an address at St. Paul's Seminary, where I still live most of the time. I also spent my "political" years here. In those days, I used to live at St. Stephen's parish in Old Chelsea, Quebec. I was happy to be there and I was only 15 minutes from the House of Commons. Each day I drove to Ottawa down Highway 5, a freeway that had been cut down into the soil to bypass Hull. On each side of the road were layers of black, grey, and white strata. A geologist friend told me that the layers represented 400 dried-up oceans. I always knew that when I got into the House and went to caucus to see what questions would be asked that day and who would ask them, everybody would be claiming that their question was essential and had to have priority. At the same time I knew that hardly anybody would remember the questions we had asked the day before, and I also knew it had taken a long time for 400 oceans to dry up.

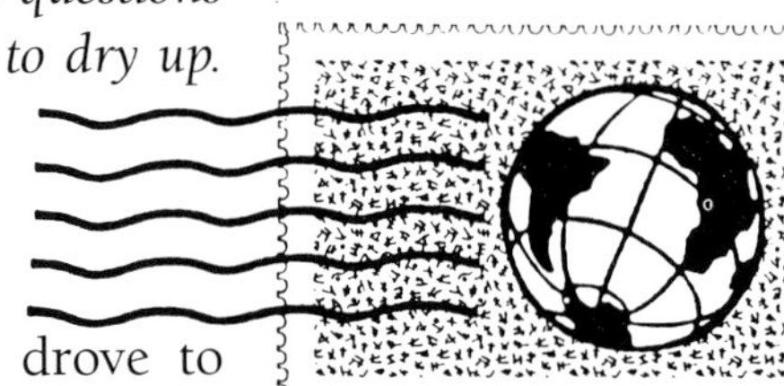

Ottawa, Canada
February 1, 1976

Before Midnight Mass, as my Christmas Eve birthday was coming to an end, I drove to Parliament Hill. At Canada's heart, "Not a creature was stirring, not even a mouse . . ." A sharp wind from the Gatineaus snapped the flag on the Peace Tower. The night was crystal clear and bone-chillingly cold. The perpetual Centennial flame to the provinces was still being fired by Alberta gas, but it did little to warm the weather. The solitary, bundled mountie who had drawn guard duty at the main door wished he were home.

Ghosts of Christmas Past reminded me of Samuel de Champlain, whose statue stands behind the Parliament Buildings and looks down on the great river that he first traversed in 1609. The Jesuits Brébeuf and Lalemant used the same Indian waterway on their journey to Fort St. Marie and their first and final mission. Long-forgotten furtraders brought thousands of pelts to wealthy dealers in Montreal on these same waters. I doubt that any of them even dreamed that one day the Gothic outlines of Canada's first capital would crown the cliff a few miles from where the Gatineau River from the north and the Rideau River from the south join the mighty Ottawa.

As a matter of fact, there was no permanent settlement here until the Napoleonic blockade ended Britain's supply of squared timber from the Baltic. To exploit the vast stands of white and red pine, Philemon Wright and his followers arrived in 1800 from Massachusetts, settling on the north side of the Chaudière Falls to found what is now the city of Hull.

Settlement on the south shore lagged until 1826 when Colonel John By of the Royal Engineers began to construct the Rideau Canal as a military route from the Ottawa River to Kingston. Thousands of Ottawa citizens now enjoy it as the longest skating rink in the world. Bytown grew rapidly, but the timber trade and the harnessing of the Chaudière to run great saw mills gave Hull the upper hand.

In 1857, Queen Victoria chose Bytown, now incorporated as the city of Ottawa, as the capital for the Province of Canada. The military encampment of Barrack Hill became the site of the Parliament Buildings. Confederation of the North American provinces in 1867 promised a great future. Growth was steady but unspectacular until the Second World War. A sudden burst of wartime building and an influx of civil servants permanently affected the economic, physical, and social development of the National Capital Region.

The new 16-storey office building housing the International Development Research Centre at 60 Queen Street is one of many which have changed the skyline in recent years. A stone's throw from the National War Memorial, it looks out upon the Peace Tower and the East Block. The bong, *bong*, ***bong***, **bong** of the clock bells at 15-minute intervals reassures us that the country is still ticking.

People often ask me how my "work" is going. It made me reflect a good deal on what that four-letter word means to different people: to farm, to fish, to clean, to mine, to smelt, to read, to write, to lumber, to teach, to listen, to cure, to think, to build, to drive, to paint, to draw, to reign, to sell, to sail, to buy, to cook, to type, to wash, to guide, to mend, to sing, . . . but it also means to put in time—something I have witnessed in many places and offices these past few weeks. To arrive at a place and endure the hours made up of

Father Bob on Parliament Hill

useless things that have become dully routine, of details that have become key issues, of water fountains and washrooms, of walking here and walking there with this piece of paper or that piece of paper. People and plans are withering under the stress of doing nothing original. Office buildings with phones and typewriters and desks and artificial plants seem to be all the same whether they are church or secular, political or business.

As for my work . . . so far, very positive. I have visited 24 different groups and have had good receptions from interesting people. When you receive this I should be on my way to India and Sri Lanka (Ceylon). During the coming months, I hope to visit clinics and training centres, drinking water and irrigation schemes, co-ops and poultry farms. In talking to and visiting with the people at the sites, I hope to find out how Canadians have aided or harassed them, to hear their suggestions, their advice. To identify these projects I have been through many basements and many files.

In the past month, I spent a few days in Western Canada. I visited funding agencies, renewed contacts with family and friends, took medical and dental checks, tenderly guarded two, fat, sore arms full of shots to ward off tropical bugs, and passed time with an ailing buddy at Mayo.

I found that prairie people take for granted one of the most inspiring sights on the planet . . . a prairie winter dawn. On several early-morning drives I had the chance to be part of the spectacle . . . The northern lights have just left centre stage and the pre-dawn blackness tingles and crunches in the icy cold. Stars hang out. The world is still. Suddenly a silent overture of hazy light breaks the southeastern horizon. Time passes. The sun struggles to break night's grasp. Slowly the haze turns to yellow, to yellow-red, to pink, to pink-yellow, to red, to red-pink-yellow. A crescendo of every colour in the spectrum floods the skies. Clouds blaze in a moment of glory. Telephone poles, hunchbacked elevators, taut fences, and frosty roofs silhouette against the morning sky. Everything is new. Not once in the last five billion years has it been just like this. Our star breaks the earth line! Darkness-light, old-new, despair-hope, death-life . . . our mysteries. Silent awe. And if you miss today's performance, there will be a new show tomorrow.

As I write these lines before leaving for the Orient, I share with you some passages from the Vatican II Document, *The Church in the Modern World*. The fifth chapter deals with the fostering of peace and the promotion of a community of nations:

> Today the bonds of mutual dependence become increasingly close between all citizens and all the peoples of the world . . . for the attainment of these goals, agencies of the international community should do their part to provide for the various necessities of men . . . Without being inflexible and completely uniform, the collection and distribution of aid should be conducted in an orderly fashion in dioceses, nations and throughout the entire world. Wherever it seems appropriate, this activity of Catholics should be carried on in unison with other Christian brothers . . .

The handbook that the Mennonites give their overseas personnel has thoughts from St. Paul put into a 20th-century mould. For lack of space, I pick only these few:

> We may speak the language of sacrifice and of service, but if we have no love in our hearts for those whom we seek to help, our efforts will have no more effect than a noisy gong or a clanging cymbal whose influence fades away with its clamor.
>
> We may emphasize the urgency of development, comprehend all the urgent problems and needs of the world, and have such absolute faith and determination that we can imagine the masses living in prosperous communities on a respectable standard of living, but if we have no love for the people, it is all in vain.
>
> Love never gives up. As for technology, it will be superseded; as for agencies of development, they will cease. For our technology and our planning and our institutions are incomplete but when our actions are guided by love and justice, then they will be complete . . .

Good stuff, think ye not? During the past two months I enjoyed the hospitality of four Canadian seminaries. At a superficial glance, the seminarians are older, fatter, and freer from rules than in the days of yore. The bishops of 2000 are somewhere among them. Good luck! Pray for me.

Love,

Roberto

India

"India still uses the world's most effective food producer – a woman with a hoe."

Sometimes life requires great leaps. From St. Philip's in Saskatoon, where I had been a parish priest, to New Delhi was one such leap. The day in 1986 when I was informed that I had a brain tumour was not unlike that trip to Delhi. Things would never be the same again. After the tests at the Princess Margaret hospital in Toronto, where the tumour was confirmed, I took the streetcar across the city to the house of a friend, Sue Hudon, who would drive me to the airport for the trip back to Ottawa. I remember the day in great detail. My senses stretched out. Before I arrived at Sue's house I had been able to hear the sound of the birds singing, over the rumble of the streetcar. That had never happened to me before because I never had time to listen.

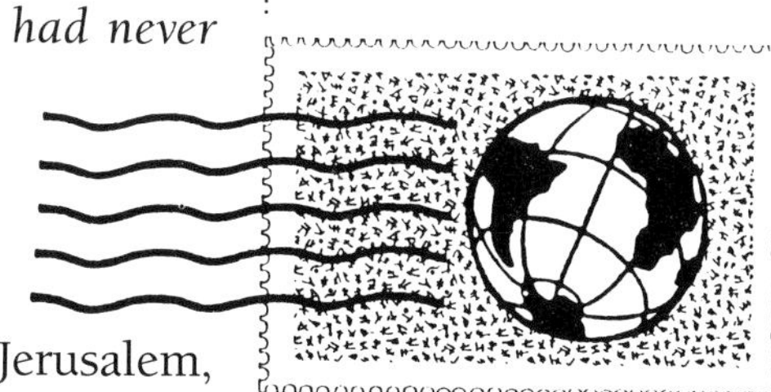

New Delhi, India
March 1, 1976

A long-time resident of Jerusalem told me, "After four days you can write a book about Jerusalem, after a month an essay, after a year a few words, after a lifetime nothing, because then you know that Jerusalem is a mystery." I feel the same is true about India. At the moment I am at the book stage.

This is being written in New Delhi, the capital of India. Giant Boeing steps brought me here. From Montreal to the antiseptic, grey, huge dullness which is Charles de Gaulle was the first step. The aircraft, bars, plastics, boutiques, aloneness, muffled talk, bedraggled clothes, garbled announcements, x-ray scanning, security, and canned music give an impression of a Universal Nowhere. Charles de Gaulle works more efficiently than most airports though. It was only the people I met at Paris, Rome, Jerusalem, and Teheran that made the journey a human adventure.

Delhi bears testimony to the legendary age of the Mahabharata epic when wars were fought between gods and heroes almost 3,000 years ago. The city lies between the Aravalli Hills to the south and northwest, and the River Yumuna to the east. Delhi's strategic position is something that no king or conqueror has ever overlooked. The city has seen the passing of many dynasties and has absorbed many cultures. In 1504 Sultan Siklander Lodi moved his court to Agra, 100 miles to the southeast. For 150 years the centre of power alternated between the two cities, finally returning to Delhi – but leaving the Taj Mahal in Agra.

By the 18th century British influence, exercised through the East India Company, was gradually increasing. This continued until 1857 when the rising against the British triggered the end of Moghul rule in India. For the next 100 years, Delhi was of secondary importance to Calcutta, the capital of British India. Under George V, government was transferred back to a recently constructed, magnificent capital called New Delhi. Today, near the river in Delhi, a simple stone platform marks the site where Mahatma Gandhi was cremated on January 31, 1948. A fanatic shot him, only months after the peaceful struggle he led brought home rule to India. Another Gandhi is in charge today.

To get to India meant an overnight stay in Paris with my French-teaching friends. In Rome, there was a Papal audience and back-home connections through Oblates and Sion. From Rome to Jerusalem was a reverse direction Peter-Paul journey to the place where the Christian schism began.

"On the Holy Mountain is His city cherished by the Lord. The Lord prefers the gates of Zion to all Jacob's dwellings. Of you are told glorious things, O city of God!" Psalm 87. Truly Jerusalem is unique and to pass a Sabbath there is unforgettable. The Temple Wall, the day of rest, the synagogue, the prayer bring Judaism alive and reaffirm that, "I am your God and you are my People." But the Jewish-Christian-Moslem tension reaffirms that humanity is divided. "I am right and you are wrong," is symbolized by the three holy days each week: Friday for the Moslems, Saturday for the Jews, Sunday for the Christians.

The weary faces of the young Israeli soldiers point to a kind of dull, universal tiredness that is the result of a long struggle. Probably the most outstanding thing for me was the Saskatoon Sisters of Sion in Jerusalem. One of their houses is the "Ecce Homo" on the Via Dolorosa, the traditional Way of the Cross. Let us simply say, that some people have come a long way since they left the Saskatoon West Side.

At the moment, I am experiencing a phenomenon which I call, "instant illiteracy." As soon as one passes the safe confines of Western Europe he becomes an illiterate. Twenty-two years of formal *education* dissolve and I stand like a three-year-old before the written word. Not only do I not understand the speech, I cannot even read the letters. Hebrew, Arabic, Persian, Sanskrit, Hindi, Chinese, Japanese are just "so much Greek to me."

Being neither officially employed by either the Church or the government, I am, in a sense, neither fish, flesh, nor fowl. But being Canadian means I can call upon the Canadian High Commission, which is Canada's embassy here. The embassies are lined up like pavilions at a world fair. Canada's building is new, a concrete elegance around a central feature of flowing water. A specially uniformed Kipling-type Indian sentry snaps a salute as you enter the grounds. I was wondering, and didn't find out, if he had any kind of unemployment insurance.

Embassies and embassy people have always been a bit mysterious to me. I have visited about 25 setups around the world. It always seems as if the people there are afraid that you have lost your passport or that one of your friends has been picked up on an opium charge . . . something that could mess up their five-hour day. If you really only want to sign the visitors' book, look for mail, or peruse a month-old *Globe and Mail*, you're welcome!

In each there is a sacred hierarchy of ambassador, diplomatic minister, minister counsellor, first secretary, second secretary, third secretary, attachés . . . the last is like a curate. The clerks, etc., who come after are the acolytes. In the High Commission here, there are 42 Canadians of whom 18 are "diplomats." The rest are "support" staff who are further supported by about 80 local people. The main areas of work include politics, development, commerce, immigration, and administration. A staffer volunteered that the life of an international civil servant moving from one country to another every two years was a life in which you were neither *in* nor *out*. You didn't know Canada and you didn't know your mission. He compared it to the rings of Saturn—concentric circles which never touch the surface.

Here the welcome was of a special kind. The high commissioner and his delightful wife asked me to dinner in their elegant home, Canada House. This was due in part to mutual back-home friends, but it's the kind of thing that someone born in Rosetown would expect of someone born in Moose Jaw. The high commissioner to Sri Lanka, a lady, is also from Moose Jaw.

Canada's aid program to India goes on even though there was a shutdown and some "naughty-naughties" when the nuclear power reactor produced an Indian atomic bomb in May 1974. India receives about one-tenth of Canada's foreign aid. In reality it is only a drop in the bucket in relation to the need.

Every sixth baby born in the world is an Indian. The Indian population was reported in the press this month as being 604 million. For those in development work, somebody has said that every problem is multiplied by 604 million . . . therefore *Big Problems!* But every solution is divided by 604 million . . . therefore *Small Solutions!* When you receive this, I should be visiting some of the small solutions in a few of the 270,000 villages in India.

Here's something that might win some bets in the beer parlour in Delisle, Saskatchewan. An official from the high commission, using U.N. reports, pointed out to me that in 1974 the world produced 361 million tons of wheat. Of that, India produced 101 million tons. Canada trailed with only 14 million tons, of which 9 million tons were exported, making it one of the highest exporters but a relatively small producer. India still uses the world's most effective food producer—a woman with a hoe. John Deere and Massey Harris would have another opinion, I'm sure.

CARITAS India has been my host agency here. It is a member of the International Conference of Catholic Charities and has consultative status with UNICEF and FAO of the United Nations. It cooperates with and distributes funds from Australia, Austria, Belgium, Britain, Canada, New Zealand, United States, Germany, Holland, Switzerland, Italy, Luxembourg, France, and Ireland. I have been impressed with their complicated but efficient operation.

Shalom,

Roberto

India

"The deep, dark, brown eyes of India have not really divulged any of their secrets."

Third World living has been part of my life. Kerala is a Third World situation but has been affected in an interesting way by the "First" World. It is the most Christian state of India due in large part to the work of European missionaries who came and baptized thousands in the 16th century. Today I live with Kerala students in Ottawa. Some of them will become missionaries in India. When I travelled through India in 1976, I met many Kerala missionaries in other states of India. Today the sensitivities to language and culture are emphasized much more than in the time of St. Francis Xavier and the early missionaries. International human rights demand a greater respect for other religions and their beliefs and practices.

As the world's population continues to explode, I think there will be less emphasis on numbers of baptisms and more on the vital signs of Christian living.

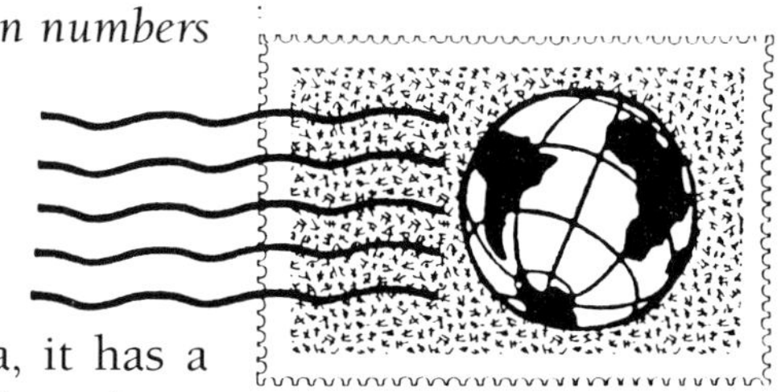

Kerala State, South India
April 1, 1976

Kerala State is in the southwest corner of India. Smaller in size than Nova Scotia, it has a population greater than Canada. The density is over 1,500 per square mile, almost four times the Indian average. It is the "Christian" state, if there is such a thing. Twenty-two per cent of the population in Kerala are Christians, whereas Christians only make up two per cent of the overall Indian population. Kerala has the highest literacy rate in India–over 60 per cent–due in some respects to the presence of the missionaries.

The Christians are divided into many rites and groups. The main Catholic rite is the Syrian-Malabar. There are also Nestorians, Jacobites, Protestants, and upper- and lower-caste Latins. Most of the people of Kerala call themselves "Thomas" Christians, dating their origins to the Apostle Thomas. I met a Jewish gentleman in a "Misereor" dentist's chair who claimed that his family predated the arrival of Thomas and that it was from their synagogue that the first Christian community was formed.

For the last three weeks, I have travelled the state by overcrowded bus, railway coach (on broad, metre, and narrow gauge), motorcycle, canoe, rickshaw, ferry, and taxi. The projects have taken me from the range of mountains that cuts Kerala off from the central plains, to the clammy heat of the tropical coastal regions. It is mid-summer, burning hot and dry. I saw the full moon of March over Calicut–that's not Calcutta. Everyone waits for the monsoons which are due in June.

The deep, dark, brown eyes of India have not really divulged any of their secrets. They have been friendly eyes, though, and what I write is what I have seen through my

Saskatchewan-blues. There are many things I could talk about, and I think that I have the basis for many long winter-night stories. India has been something like a giant midway. Everyone who walks a midway sees it in a different light. There are no two instants exactly the same.

The first overall impression is the quiet dignity of a handsome people. The second has been rather more startling. I have found India much more like South America than I could ever have imagined. In the rural areas (and 80 per cent of the population still live in the villages), it seems there are more similarities than differences. The "Culture of Poverty" has a universality about it, as does the "Culture of Opulence." The Taj Mahal International Hotel in Bombay could be in San Francisco, Tokyo, Paris, or Johannesburg. The life in the hotel may as well be on another planet.

In the villages I encountered many familiar sights and practices: the mud houses, the earthen pots, the carried water, the open, smoky fires, the simple basic foods, the lack of tomorrow's security, the sacrificial prayer and offerings for good weather, the simple festivals to celebrate life and death, the fear of strangers – be they Indian or foreign, the beasts of burden – oxen, donkeys, and humans, the creak of carts, the endless waiting, the broiling sun, the tired feet . . . None of these have geographical boundaries.

The slums are another reality. Built up on useless land or garbage dumps, they bring together the dispossessed. Born someplace else, migrants come together in what can only be described as hordes. Packed into the squalor of shacks made from packing crates, sacking, cardboard boxes, and flattened tin cans, people know new pressures: the pressures of the world's poor. Open sewers carry the refuse, flies carry the diseases, broken cultural and family patterns carry the human sorrow. This is true in Lima, Rio de Janeiro, Dakar, or Manila.

Several times in my life, I have made a very short but profound acquaintance with a person. One such incident happened at Indore in the state of Madhya Pradesh. This is a place where the United Church of Canada has left a deep impression over the years. Two of the projects I intended to visit were there. My plans were to leave there on a Saturday.

Early on Friday morning, an old German SVD Brother with a sun helmet, a hefty girth, a long white beard, and 40 years of experience in India introduced me to a Dr. Nagu. The German and this doctor, who was a Hindu from the Brahman caste, had worked together on a program for the lepers. Lepers in India are treated much as they were in Biblical times. They are driven from their villages and have to wander as lost souls. Leprosy is associated with sin and evil. Brahmans usually have nothing to do with them. Through his friendship with the Brother, Dr. Nagu had given over his life to the care of the poor and the lepers. On Saturday evening there was to be a first-year anniversary celebration of a prayer room that had been set up in a leper colony. Dr. Nagu asked me to go with him. I accepted and changed my travel plans to Sunday.

Early on Saturday morning the local newspaper arrived, and on the front page was Dr. Nagu's

India

picture. I could not read the Hindu but I was told that it was his death notice. He had died the previous evening; so instead of the celebration for the lepers, he would be going to the funeral pyre. Immediately after death, a Hindu's body is placed on the ground behind his house. Friends come to pay respects. Within the day there is a religious ceremony with the symbols of the Hindu faith. Then the men carry the body to the place where it will be burned. The women stay to mourn at the home. The body is placed on a high pile of dry firewood. The eldest son lights the torch and the flames leap up. Then there is an "hour of condolence," when the men sit around near the fire and speak about the deceased. I was asked to say a few words in English. At the end, little pieces of wood and a flower are given to each person to throw on the fire. It will burn all night and the next day the ashes are swept up to be carried to a sacred river where they will be thrown into the flowing water.

The German Brother told me that two days before the doctor's death, they had had a long talk on death and the hereafter. The German was holding out for a German heaven, the doctor was counting on reincarnation. A big Bavarian hand pointed upwards. "Now he knows!" said the Brother.

A 12-hour bus ride south of Bombay is Goa. It has a special story to tell. Colonized by the Portuguese in the late 15th century, Goa remained under their control until it was "liberated" in 1961. Swaying coconut palms, a special liquor made from the cashew nut, crumbling Baroque churches, and the Portuguese language would lead one to believe that you were in northeast Brazil rather than Asia. Goa has been a great exporter of priests and bishops to the rest of India. In one of the churches is the body of St. Francis Xavier, the Jesuit missionary of Asia. He had done his "thing" before he was 46. Prior to his death, he was credited with having baptized more than 700,000 converts. His baptizing arm is in the Jesu Church in Rome, the rest of his bones are in Goa.

In a visit to a local village parish, I found a crusty, old painting of a long-since-dead cleric. He was Dom Mateus de Castro de Alcunha Machado, and in my hunt for the greatest loser, he received a lot of points. He was the first native Goan bishop and he was born in that village. Below the painting, written in ancient Portuguese, was an outline of his life, roughly translated as follows: "In defence of his jurisdiction (authority and power) against the Jesuits, he went three times to Rome (around South Africa). He died in 1679 on his trip back home but he had received more jurisdiction . . ." Great loser!

In most Third World countries, trucks are special beings. Each is an individual, painted and marked by the owner with designs and sayings which make it unique. On St. Patrick's Day I was jam-packed into a steaming bus traversing a mountain gorge, the only Celt aboard and not even a possibility of a "piper's horn." With a sore back, no drinking water, caught in a real down-to-earth population explosion, mentally struggling with problems of unemployment, hunger, violence, economic incentives, rate of growth, etc., there was suddenly an old truck in front of us. It was painted purple and on the back, surrounded by pink flowers, printed in red, white, and blue were the words, "BE HAPPY." No way to beat that kind of spirit, is there? And that's not an April Fool joke either.

Abraços,

Roberto

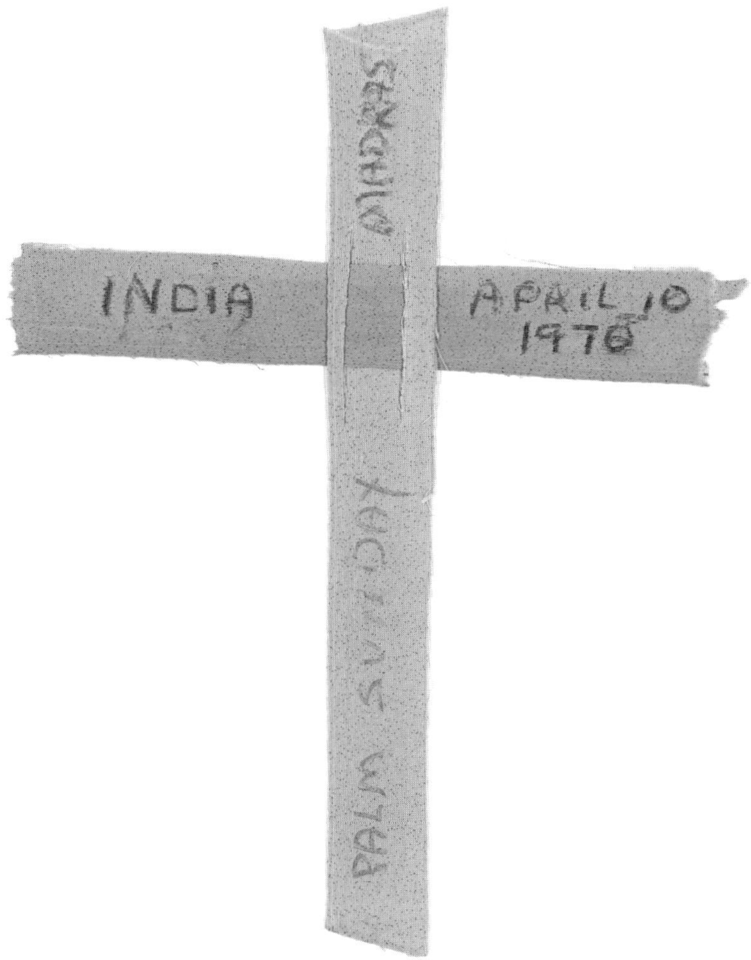

Handmade by Father Bob while in India

"Travelling on this road is no joke."

Calcutta has left a deep impression on me. It is unique. No matter where I go, Calcutta remains different. It has inspired me. Bengali people are extraordinary. They are ready to confront the impossible and come away from it with dignity. When things have been difficult for me in Parliament, Church, or illness, I remember those dark eyes and sombre faces. Nothing is impossible. In Bangladesh with the North-South committee, I met the same Bengalis. I had been told that Bangladesh was a basket case, but I found a noble people, hard working, ingenious, who had been dealt a poor hand. I often hear people in our culture say, "If they would only work they would be well off." LIES! *The hardest workers in the world, sugar-cane cutters, are the poorest. The soft, lazy, stock and bond coupon cutters are the richest.*

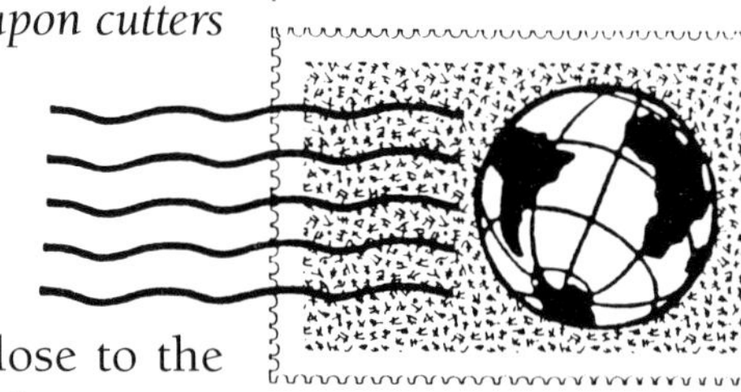

Calcutta, India
May 1, 1976

Calcutta is Mother Teresa country. If the world were a barrel, this city would be close to the bottom. A few monuments remain to the past glory of the capital of British India, but the misery in the streets is what strikes the traveller most. One wonders how much longer anybody can hold the lid on the pot. Today is May Day, and without a doubt the pot will seethe.

Easter morn broke for me at Darjeeling, a hill station looking onto the eternal snows of the Himalayas. Canadian Jesuits have been there for over 30 years. Lent, which began for me at Nasik, some 300 miles northeast of Bombay, was a new and different experience in every way. The Ash Wednesday liturgy was unique. I did not understand the language (Marahati), the music was played on a stringed instrument I had never heard before, the gestures and postures were unfamiliar (we sat barefooted on the floor), the images and symbols in the little church were Indian and strange. Yet I felt completely at home. This would shake the old argument that the Mass must be in Latin to preserve our unity. I knew that I shared the faith of those I was with, and in the signs of Bread and Wine, I remembered that, "As often as you do these things, you shall do them in memory of Me."

It is impossible to recount the events of these past two months. Some have asked that I try to describe a typical day. The following is a part of my "longest" day. Names and project numbers have been changed to protect the innocent.

. . . The night has been hot, and the straw mattress I have placed on the floor is soaking with sweat. It is my 38th sleeping place since I left Ottawa. It is still dark but dawn will break sharply at 6:00 A.M. The first sound I hear is the *swish*, swish, *swish* of a large, rusty ceiling fan which has kept most of the nighttime mosquitoes away. I have a pail of water to bathe,

Statue of Gandhi, India

shave, and what-have-you. At 6:00 I join Father Thome at a local novitiate for a concelebrated Mass. Fifty barefoot novices assist and sing Joe Wise songs. Thome has guided me around for the last few days. He is a symbol of real development. Past 60, he is still a ball of energy. He squints through friendly eyes and has close-cropped white hair and uneven buck teeth. The years have not drained his energy and he has accepted with a smile life for what it is–a mess!

A strange mixture of rice and vegetables along with lukewarm coffee in a cracked cup is breakfast. At 7:15, the 1951 jeep which defies further repairs has to be pushed to start. That's a bad omen, but it sputters to life and we are off. It is only then that Thome tells me he has just learned to drive, and the full turn of slack in the steering wheel makes me wonder if I will see the sun go down again. The price of a tank of gas at a filling station is equal to a working man's wages for six weeks. The road is already busy: oxcarts, bicycles, buses, trucks, and a steady stream of pedestrians on both sides. We *horn* our way through, sometimes to the right, sometimes to the left, missing buses with miracle passes, scattering goats and sheep, and always giving way to cows rather than humans. I hold on with both hands and wonder what real effect the St. Christopher medal has.

By 10:00 the temperature is over 100. We arrive at *India 70C/49P–Land Settlement Scheme for Refugees, $6,245*. It is a hot, dry, burned-out 75 acres. Original plans were to place 20 Tamil refugee families from Sri Lanka there. Two years have passed without a drop of rain. Five wells have been hand-dug, but no pump-sets have been installed. A small chicken scheme went on the rocks. A grape vineyard shows a bit of promise. It is being irrigated by the only well that has a bit of water. A hand tractor has been rigged up to run a small pump. There are no refugees, no houses. At another site some houses have been built, but most of the people have abandoned them because of the drought. It is a real *Grapes of Wrath* situation. We find a family: a 30-year-old father, his wife, and three children. They eke out a living from a little garden which they water from the well. I can't help but notice the look in the wife's eyes when her husband talks to us. They say, "He's the greatest man alive."

We move on to see the local cleric. He is youngish and a little slow. His living conditions are tough. His house is full of skinny rabbits and rabbit turds. He is building a new marble altar in his church. Our jeep won't start so we rent another car to see *Project 71 C/43N–Irrigation Project of Seven Wells, $7,434*. The wells had been dug and pumps were installed. One well is dry but the others have an hour of dirty water per day. Thome pushes the green slime aside and draws a drink with a pail. I say that I'm not thirsty. The farmers each have about an acre of peanuts. Their fields stand out like green carpets surrounded by red concrete. The project was supposed to start a revolving fund with the farmers paying back loans so that more wells could be dug. Payment has been poor because of the drought and because the Church has always been looked upon as a handout organization. Thome sees the good side, "When the rains come back, the wells will be good and they *are dug* now."

We go back to the cleric's house for lunch. We have rice, curry, and one of the rabbits. The other rabbits sit around our feet for the crumbs. There are no crumbs. I am given two bottles of soda water to drink. I don't really trust it, but I drink them anyway. Almost everything has been diluted along the way, even soda water. It is hot but it is water.

A local mechanic has taken the starter off the jeep and "fixed" the motor. He charges four rupees. We push it again and it starts. We head out for *India 64 A/23 N Dairy-Sheep Scheme, $2,400*. In a little while the jeep stops again. The clutch is gone, there is no starter, and the throttle linkage has come apart. I suggest we hitchhike. We park the heap and get a ride on a loaded truck with a steaming radiator. The crowd on top make room for us in the mid-afternoon sun.

A mile from the project site we get down and walk to the thatched village. My arrival draws a crowd like a Barnum and Bailey show. The local pastor has thick glasses, snow white hair and beard, a pot belly, and a dirty cassock. He welcomes us and in the first five minutes introduces me to his 25-year-old cook and wonders if I can get some money for the cook to get married. We meet his 11-year-old seminary prospect, and find out that the parish is really in tune with Vatican II because it only has one main statue in the church.

Project 64 A/23N was to give a loan to 10 farmers to buy sheep or cows. After a year each would give a calf or lamb back to the project. The animal would then be given to another family. Word was sent out to the farmers to come and describe their operation. Only one appears. I have a suspicion that the other nine suspect a loan collector. This man explains that he bought a water buffalo for 800 rupees. She was sick so he got rid of her by trading up for a 1,000-rupee buffalo. "At first she gave four litres of milk in the morning and three litres of milk in the evening. Now there is hardly any water, so she only gives three litres all day. She has two calves: a female that is this high, and a new bull calf." He has paid back half his loan but is not ready to part with the calves. He runs a tea-house so he uses the milk in his tea. He then sends out to bring us a glass of tea. It is warm and has a good mixture of buffalo milk.

None of the other farmers are in the village, but the daughter of one has been collected. I feel like a heel. She seems like the "token maid," a Susanna before her judges. There are 50 people in the house and 500 outside. The girl is 18, an Indian beauty, tall and dark, barefoot, nervous but calm. Her shiny black hair hangs in a long braid down her back and over her dirty sari. She is the oldest of nine. She has been to school and is waiting to be married, but her family cannot afford the dowry. Her father had bought 10 sheep with his loan. They have had 30 lambs in the last three years, "sometimes one, sometimes two, sometimes three." They have paid back a bit of the loan but the sheep have been used to keep the family alive. The pastor

India

Bathers in the Ganges, India

tells me, “They will pay it all back before she gets married. I’ll see to that.” I figure it’s time we move on. We walk to the road and wait in the darkness for a ride back to base. Thome has supper in a crowded roadside stand. I’m starving but decide to wait for tomorrow. At 12:30 I’m back on the mattress . . . *swish,* swish, *swish*.

. . . Trivia: There are no spray cans in India. Nobody is worried about whether the chlorofluorocarbons will hurt the ozone layer. How many spray cans do you need? On my way up the snakelike mountain road to Darjeeling, the taxi had to stop for repairs five times. A 10-year-old Bengali boy riding in the same car tried his English on me and said, “Travelling on this road is no joke!” That about sums it up.

Roberto

“. . . one thing I am sure of: the people of India are the only ones who can solve the problem.”

I am glad that I have been around the world several times: I know how small it is. And these last years have taught me just how fragile our existence is. We are all interrelated. Anything you or I do will have an influence on all our sisters and brothers around the globe. More than half the resources consumed in the entire history of the planet have been used up in my lifetime. Most of the pollution destroying creation has occurred since my father was born. Fifteen billion years of creation destroyed by two generations! I have decided that as long as I live and am able to function, I will address that question.

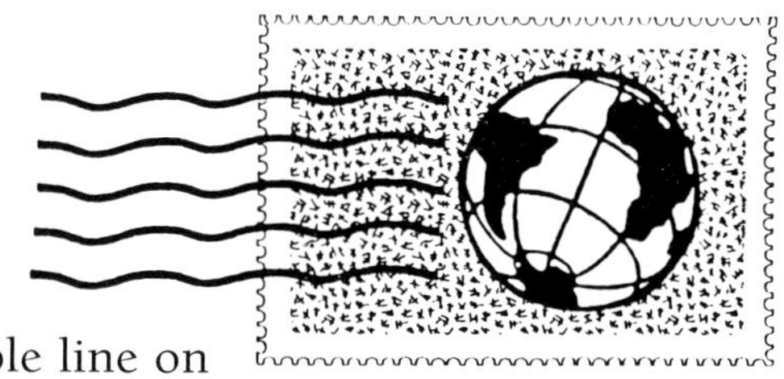

International Date Line
Pacific Ocean
June 1, 1976

Just east of the Fiji Islands in the western Pacific is the 180th meridian. This invisible line on the globe is exactly opposite of the Greenwich meridian in England. This is the spot where new days begin, where Mondays become Tuesdays. Going east from here, one gains a day, going west one loses a day. So coming home, I picked up an extra day . . . one more morning to wake up. Now I have a problem: 1976 already has 366 days. Do I have 367 because I went around the world?

I hopscotched across Australia on my way back to Canada. The eight-and-one-half-hour Bombay flight dropped me off at Perth, Western Australia, and from there I did a kind of Vancouver, Winnipeg, Toronto, Ottawa, Montreal trip through Adelaide, Melbourne, Canberra, and Sydney. The headquarters for the “Asian Fund for Human Development” is in Sydney. For the last three years the Canadian Organization for Development and Peace, along with other international organizations, has funded this group directly, and CCODP is responsible for deciding which projects in southeast Asia will receive assistance.

Australia is a huge, rambunctious, empty country with modern cities and a short history. Right now it is enjoying our type of October-like, Indian-summer weather. A nation of sportsmen and gamblers, many Australians look like they are characters out of a Clipper Ship movie. All seem to have just run a mile and drunk a beer. Australia is still reeling over the political upheaval of the last six months. Nineteen per cent of the population were born outside the country. An old lady on a bus told me, “You scarcely hear Australian on the streets any more.” She was at least partly right. An Italian taxi driver (with an Australian accent over the Italian dialect) reflected, “I no alika thisa city . . . I lika mucha mora Roma.” Some new-found friends got me a pass to

India

the Speakers Gallery in the Canberra Parliament. I didn't have the proper coat and tie, so a civil servant stripped his own off right there in the entrance and gave them to me. He was overheard saying to a friend, "There's a bloody Yank priest in here who stands bloody six foot five and weighs bloody 16 stone. He's got my bloody jumper on and if he moves his bloody arms he'll tear the bloody seam right down the bloody back." I felt confident that the old lady didn't have anything to worry about.

I spent my last night in India in the Bombay airport. My flight from London arrived four hours late and during the interval, three 747s were loaded for Europe. All facilities were overtaxed in the 100 degree heat. At that time I noted that, "I was hot, sticky, and tired, not with the tiredness of a hard job done, but the tiredness of a very long wait in a sweltering, crowded airport late at night. I was a bit edgy with the tensions that come from the *customs' formalities* of a developing country. It was three months to the hour since I began my Indian journey and there was a certain satisfaction in having come and seen and lasted. I doubted if I would ever be the same again. Even a short time in rural India puts a different perspective on everything."

June 1st marks the halfway point of my year with the International Development Research Centre. It is hard to say what I have learned or how I have changed. I trust that while I am back in Canada, I will have a chance to see many of you so that you can help with my debriefing.

One thing I did find out is that my old bag of bones is still able to take quite a bit of punishment. Actually, it is not that difficult, as long as one keeps a few rules in mind, i.e., Even if you're hungry, never eat it unless you are sure . . . Even if you're thirsty, never drink it unless you are sure . . . Never, never forget your malaria pills . . . Keep your head down if the West Bengalis are having a demonstration . . . Bananas and peanuts are always safe to eat; beer if you can find it, is always safe to drink.

Finally, toward the end of my Indian experience, I found I no longer had a norm from which to judge things. I had come so close to the situation that my original norms were blending into the local reality. An agronomist from the International Development Research Centre, that I met along the way, told me, "When that happens, it is time to go home and reestablish your norms."

June also marks the first anniversary of the "state of emergency" in India. A year ago the Congress party led by Mrs. Gandhi suspended democratic rights, took over a strict censorship of the press, and arrested most of the opposition. She has been receiving a bad Western press. It is not really so easy to say what she should have done. It seems that the country had fallen into real anarchy. Prices were skyrocketing, trains and public transportation had just about ceased to move, factories were closed, and construction had ground to a halt. Many Indians believe that things are better now. Food prices have dropped 20 per cent and things are running . . . more or less. I would hazard a guess that India has been in a kind of state of emergency for the last 1,000 years or so and it has finally been called by name. I do not have a clue what could or should be done, but one thing I am sure of: the people of India are the only ones who can solve the problem.

Calcutta was my hub for about four weeks. I had a room at the archbishop's house, a great rambling monstrosity of a place built in the 19th century. Its thick walls broke a bit of the Bengali heat, but even at night, temperatures remained in the high 90s. From Calcutta I took four trips: to the northeast, the north, the northwest, and the west. I suppose I would have headed south too, except that to the south, there is only the Ganges Delta and the Bay of Bengal. The next stop is Antarctica. I was particularly impressed with the people who stay at the "Razor's Edge" – those who have decided that they will put their lives on the line for the poor, the dispossessed, the sick, the hungry, the dying, whether it is in the slums of Calcutta or in the Hill Stations among the Tribals. While I was in Calcutta, the archbishop, the tallest Indian I met and a most gracious man, was made a cardinal. He is the president of the Bishops' Conference in India and we had several long talks about the state of the Church there. At the moment, the forced sterilization of people who have more than two children is causing concern. The Catholic minority is protesting as are the Mohammedans. Mrs. Gandhi is in a bind. The population is still climbing by about 14 million per year, even after all the birth-control campaigns. If there was some realistic immigration policy, I don't think all the passenger ships in the world could transport the annual surplus of these human beings for resettlement each year.

Just before I returned to Calcutta on my last jaunt, I spent a 12-hour day on a dilapidated bus as I covered about 160 miles in the state of Bihar. I was told that Bihar has over 60 million inhabitants. It is not the largest state territorially in India, but it has one of the largest populations. Although it has rich resources in iron, coal, and manganese, some of which are being developed, the majority of the people eke out a miserable living from farming. May is the middle of the hot season, monsoons were a month away. River beds a half-mile wide were bone dry, vegetation had vanished except for a few trees that must have had roots a mile long and straight down. The high-pitched buzz of insects that thrive in heat, pierces your ears from morning till night.

The population of this single Indian state is larger than that of either France, Italy, or West Germany. There are more people in Bihar than in any country in South America, except Brazil. On the particular day that I mention, there was a partial eclipse of the sun. It began about 4:45 P.M. and was clearly visible until the sun sank below the horizon at about 6:10. To the Hindus, an eclipse of the sun means great disasters are in store. For the sun to set in eclipse means that even more sinister things are in the offing. Their mythology tells them that the Celestial Serpent is trying to eat the sun, which they look upon as a god. To ward off the evil, they fast and try to get to a body of water to bathe and make amends for their sins. Newspapers reported countless throngs of people from all over India travelling to the Ganges. Temples along the road were packed. As the eerie light of the eclipse spread over the land, this poor wayfaring cowboy decided

Bus stop, India

to call his final report for the I.D.R.C., *The Year the Snake Bit the Sun.*

Considering the short time I was in India and the abundance of this country's literature, it was impossible to begin any real study of Indian writing. However, I did see one little gem of an idea by Bengali poet Rabindranath Tagore. He is the composer of the Indian National Anthem. He wrote: "A teacher can never teach, unless he is still learning himself. A lamp cannot light another lamp unless it continues to burn its own flame . . . the Teacher who has come to the end of his subject, who has no living traffic with his knowledge, but merely repeats his lessons to his students can only load their minds, he cannot quicken them. Truth not only must inform but must inspire. If the inspiration dies out and the information only accumulates, then Truth loses its infinity . . . "

I hope to be in Canada for four to six weeks before starting the second part of my study in South America. During that time, I hope to see many of you.

Happy Holidays,

Roberto

"To know how many people there are has been a problem from the time of Caesar Augustus to the present."

Montreal remains a great and interesting modern city. I have travelled there many times and have taken a good number of trips into the province of Quebec. Relatives and graves of my ancestors are a constant invitation to return.

The dome of St. Joseph's Oratory still dominates the skyline of Montreal. This grandiose place of worship is a result of the faith and prayers of Brother André Bisette, who founded it. While I was a member of Parliament, I was invited to be part of a delegation to go to Rome to assist at his beatification.

Mayor Jean Drapeau of Montreal was part of our group. At dinner one evening, another delegate humorously challenged Drapeau about his years as mayor. Drapeau tactfully avoided confrontation. Then he turned to me and said, "There are two things you should never do as a politician. First, never comment on a rumour. Second, never answer a hypothetical question." Best political advice I ever received. Very few politicians ever learn it.

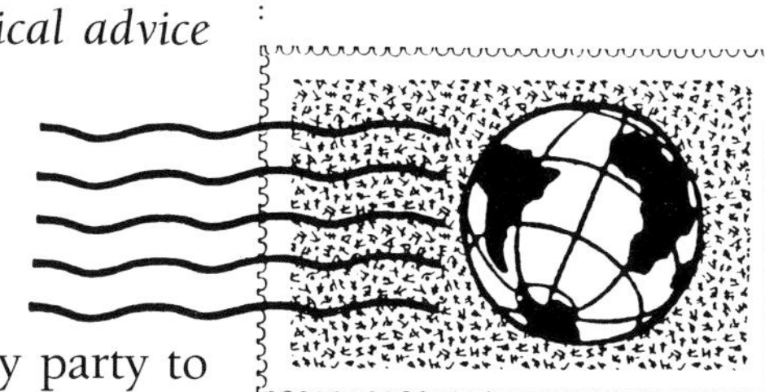

Montreal, Canada
July 1, 1976

Today is Canada's birthday. Our country is a tottery 109 years old. Another birthday party to the south celebrates our neighbour's 200th. What is the life expectancy of a country today? Summer vacationers will have little time to worry about such things.

I date-line this from Montreal, which in the minds of many around the world is the same thing as Canada. That is due, I am sure, to the genius of the local mayor, who has gained more free publicity for his city because of the Olympic building disputes than if he had 100 press agents in every country.

The Olympic Village stands waiting. Secret police from many nations are on the alert. R.C.M.P. and other Canadian gendarmes are out in droves. Sixteen thousand soldiers are on full-time duty guarding the frontiers. As an old grade-school poem goes, "Play up, Play up and Play the Game!" So far I have only met three people who have tickets to any event, although I understand that all seats are sold.

While in India, I was interviewed once by a Hindi newspaper. The interview had nothing to do with what I was doing in India but only about whether the games would go on or not, and if the Indian field-hockey team would be hindered by playing on artificial turf. As far as

Brazil

I know, the only entry from the 604 million Indians will be their hockey team of 12 players. It will take many generations to have the volunteer donations of Canadians to international development equal the cost and loss suffered by the games.

On my return journey to Ottawa I visited two Robbies, Little Robbie and Big Robbie. Little Robbie lives in the Hawaiian Islands. Big Robbie has spent the last five months at the Mayo Clinic in Rochester, Minnesota, in a courageous struggle against the inroads of cancer in his body. Big Robbie has lost a good deal of flesh but none of his fighting spirit. Little Robbie, who lives in the Rosetown-size town of Lanai on the "Pineapple Island," is full of the questions that come to little boys.

"Grandpa Ogle, where's Grandma Ogle?" My five-year-old grandson, Robert Satory Hotta, was not only wondering why he had three grandfathers, but was surprised that he had only two grandmothers.

"Things are different in Brazil, Robbie," his mother explained, and therein lies a tale.

Back in the dim distant past of our Brazilian Mission, our house was a meeting place for many of the Peace Corps volunteers who then worked in the northeast of Brazil. At Christmastime we would invite them for a North American-style Christmas dinner. At one of these gatherings, our Peace Corps man at União dos Palmares, a wandering Hawaiian whose ancestors had originated in the Land of the Rising Sun, met the Peace Corps girl from the village on the other side of the mountain. As such stories are bound to go, they romanced and were married in Brazil. Our Saskatoon team had the honour to be the celebrators of the event. Each of us had a part to play and I was the Father of the Bride. Thus it has come about that Dad is now Granddad, and Grandson Robbie is wondering about Grandma Ogle.

Each return to Canada from another land produces a kind of culture shock. Adapting back to a way of life, I find harder than adapting to a foreign style. Questions have been plentiful. "Is my money being well spent? Are the projects a success? Are they helping to solve the problem?" Western questions to Eastern situations and I find myself hard put to give a clear answer. Eastern situations are too complex for clear answers. Westerners, as a rule, want quick solutions. Easterners, from long experience, know that patience is still the key. All I have been able to do is to suggest that what is being done does have an effect but in proportion to the reality, it is almost insignificant.

And what does insignificant mean? It would be as if you tried to paint a skyscraper with a toothbrush and a cupful of paint. "How's the paint job coming?" someone asks. "Well, there it is. See for yourself," you reply. Nobody can deny that you have painted a six-by-six inch-square very well. But what about the skyscraper? That is when one hopes that with the little beginning, someone might bring a lot more toothbrushes, or maybe somebody will invent a paint sprayer or something.

The month of June has been a time of refitting. Like a weathered ship home from the sea, I have been undergoing a general overhaul, which includes baggage, clothes, notebooks, teeth, friendships, contacts, beds, food. I steamed into Vancouver as the United Nations meeting on housing, HABITAT, was beginning. Ordinarily I would have loved to participate, but I was literally too saturated and tired to stop. Mother Teresa, Barbara Ward, and Margaret Mead had a significant impact on the assembled delegates. "Let everyone have pure water . . . Love is more than words; it is sharing your goods." Simple but forthright messages. Still, political reality and how to deal with power remain burning issues. I suspect that everyone who was there had a different impression of what had happened. But in the end, it seemed that the little guys didn't like the way the big guys treated them. The possibility of having a house of one's own becomes less and less possible for the poor.

The month of June was also census time. I was in Canada but I don't think I was counted. To know how many people there are has been a problem from the time of Caesar Augustus to the present. A census is a slice of life at a particular moment. Our slice was tabulated at the place one slept on the night of May 31 to June 1. An in-law was one of the counters. There seemed to be almost as many counters as people being counted. Charts and maps and books and reports and forms and pencils were produced in abundance. Canada was interested in knowing where people had lived, what kinds of homes they had, how they were making out at their work. To the counters, people in trailer courts and motels, as well as railroad work crews, campers, and tenters proved to be problems. Computers will now tabulate and spin for five years. Final reports will not be drafted until the charts and books and forms and pencils appear again in 1981. I kept wondering how the system would work in Calcutta.

People have said, "It must be good to be in Canada." And of course it is good to be here. Some things do seem a bit shocking, though. When I see a waitress in a restaurant leave a tap running so that the water will get cold, when I use an automatic washing machine to wash my clothes, or hear a dishwasher grunt, groan, and spurt its way through barrels of water, I squirm a little bit and remember those dry river beds, those empty wells, those half-filled pots of just a few weeks ago.

But I suppose one of the biggest differences is to drive on a road in Saskatchewan, mile after mile on a road that becomes *my* road because there is not a sign of movement in front or behind. Finally, another vehicle seems like an intruder. At this time of year, verdant fields stretch horizon-wide, the parklands look like some new Eden, glorious sunsets are only minutes away from panoramic dawns. So few people to enjoy so much!

Nature has whipped the Prairies this year with devastating storms. As a kid, I knew that there were really only three dates in Prairie history. The heavy snow of '07, the big rain of '16, the cyclone of '23. Everything that had taken place was dated either before or after those events.

This summer may turn out to be another such date to the historian. Hurricane winds, slashing hail, and monsoonlike rains lashed the Prairies on several occasions. Radio towers tumbled, trailer courts were devastated, farmsteads ruined, sloughs inundated. But when the storm passed, there was that calm that is unequalled—the calm after the storm.

In mid-July, I plan to leave for Brazil. There I will attempt a program similar to what I did in India, to visit about 25 sites of projects throughout the great land beneath the Southern Cross.

Até Logo,

Roberto

India

"Somewhere out in the mystery that is death, a voice said, 'Safe.'"

In this letter, I wrote about my dad. Each time I read it, I cry. My dad is still so real to me and so much of my life is his life. A near-illiterate, he had a great grasp of life. He expressed his wisdom in very simple ways. Material things were really worthless to him; loving relations and friends were what mattered. Dad was my best friend and since his passing I have lived in a kind of vacuum. He would never have understood my political life, but it was due basically to his philosophy–that the ordinary person should have a better break–that I was there. He would not have felt that one could work for the ordinary man by becoming a "mucky-muck," his word for a person of power and prestige.

My father left me with a great handicap. He never showed me how to handle anger. I never remember anger in our home. He loved my mother to the point that on her death, he said, "Today is the only day she has ever done anything to hurt me."

Flying Down to Rio
August 1, 1976

"Safe." The word stirs one of my first childhood memories. A steaming Model T coupe putts its way into the littered garage. It is 10 hours since we began the 30-mile round trip to Mass. Two flat tires, deep headaches from long fasting, a sermon in French and English, weekend church-step news from relatives and friends, the hum of grasshoppers, the starchy smell of Sunday clothes, spirals of dust-bowl earth had all been part of the long day. Then my dad's huge but gentle hand reaches out to turn off the Magneto. The motor coughs a few more times, sputters to a stop. Only the whistle of the leaking radiator and the bawling of the cows waiting to be milked can be heard. We are all home safe. Every trip that my father took ended with that word.

Henry B. Ogle with Dorothy Ogle, Robert Ogle, and Eileen Fitzgerald

On July 8th, a few minutes after I had talked to him on the phone from Ottawa, the Eternal Hand reached out and turned off the switch on my father's heart. Somewhere out in the mystery that is death, a voice said, "Safe." Years before when he had suffered a slight heart attack, the doctor told him he would have to be careful because of his heart. "It will do me till I die," he had replied. Our stepmother was happy because his prayers had been answered. Within hours of his death, his whole family was present. The obituary column read:

OGLE, Henry Bernard. On July 8, 1976, Henry Ogle of Rivière Qui Barre, age 83 years, passed away. He leaves his loving wife Mary, two sons and two daughters. Rev. Robert Ogle, Ottawa; Charles Ogle, Coleville, Saskatchewan; Mrs. Frank (Marguerite) Kebe, and Miss Mary Lou Ogle, Calgary; seven grandchildren, also three brothers and one sister. Mass of Christian Burial was held Saturday at St. Emerence Church of Rivière Qui Barre. A son Rev. Robert Ogle officiated. Mr. Ogle was forwarded to Rosetown, Saskatchewan for funeral services and interment. Mass of Christian Burial was held Monday, July 12th, at St. Theresa's Church in Rosetown, Saskatchewan. Rev. Robert Ogle and 19 other priests were in the sanctuary. Interment followed in the Rosetown Cemetery. Connelly-McKinley Ltd., Edmonton, and Clements Funeral Home, Rosetown, were in charge of arrangements.

Obituary columns leave a lot unsaid. As I drove across the prairies with two young nieces, they were able to fill in a lot of the details. His youngest granddaughter said, "He was tall." Maybe that said it better than anything else. But they also remembered that he had snow white hair, that he came to see them every Christmas, that he travelled a lot, but liked trains the most. That he came from Quebec and spoke French and English. That he was not well educated but he sure was smart. That he knew about everything that was going on. That he lived mostly in small towns. That he tried to teach his grandchildren French. That he liked to smoke his pipe and have a drink of good Calgary water. That he was a holy man and prayed a lot. That he was quiet when he got older, but still liked to tell stories. That he had big hands and soft skin and smelled like tobacco. That he liked mail and people . . . but most of all he liked people.

For him, I'm sure his farewell Masses of Christian burial were made to order. There were lots of people. Relatives and friends came from far and wide. The gentlest of summer evenings was the setting in Qui Barre. The full moon of July was rising as the sun disappeared in a blaze of glory. Two pipers in full regalia played the Lament. Nature's peace symbolized the peace we prayed for him.

He took his last ride by train with his youngest daughter. That too was fitting. When he was young he had worked on the railroad. He never lost his love for the Iron Horse. In Rosetown, the skies were lowering, but it didn't rain. The liturgy was joyful, the community hospitality traditional, and friends and relatives were in abundance. He now rests beside my mother in the soil that the glaciers brought 100 million years ago. It was a great grace for me to be present. I was only days away from being in an Andean village in some part of South America.

Stories abounded in the gatherings which followed each one of these events. Dad had been a master of the one-liner. My sister remembered on the day of her wedding as she and Dad were about to start down the aisle: "Well, this is the last time you will ever be going anywhere with a good-looking man." My sister-in-law hadn't yet come to understand his lingo when she was told on her wedding day that, "this was a good day for the job." At my ordination banquet, he broke up an audience that was still deeply affected by my mother's recent death when he said, "I'm not very good at making speeches, the last one I made was when I graduated out of grade three." As the years wore on, his memory faded and he would tell people, "I've lost my mind, but I don't miss it much."

He spoke a language which the stranger did not know. A mixture of Gaelic, Anglo-Saxon, French, and homemade pronunciation allowed him to come up with expressions like, "Whisht your noise"; "A grousk is coming"; "The granary calved"; "Hold your Holt." Fhooty, streelish, skittery, buttany, chimley were all words that we knew the meaning of, but had no place in a dictionary.

Several years ago, I spent a night in the Montreal airport. A blizzard was raging and everything was grounded. I had an outline of the yet-unpublished book, *Limits to Growth,* a grim analysis of the technological society and the destruction of the environment. I was struck by the fact that everything that I could see and hear in the airport had not even been thought of when my father was born: the planes, the gasoline engines, the moving stairs, the artificial foods, the synthetic fabrics, the radio, television and radio waves that were penetrating space, the plastics, the neon lights. He had seen each one come, as he moved from Pontbriand, Quebec, to Gunworth, to Lenny, to Springville, to Rosetown, to Qui Barre, yet his basic values and beliefs remained unchanged. He was still Irish, Catholic, and voted Liberal. People counted, and nothing was worth a damn that did not take that into consideration. In two minutes he always knew what a person's name was, how old he was, and where he had come from.

He did enjoy pipelining with my brother because "it put him in mind off" the steam-threshing outfits of his youth.

He had a few four-letter words in his vocabulary. The worst of all was "debt." He dreaded and feared this more than death itself. The Great Depression and the burning drought of the 1930s had affected him more than any other thing in his life. A scar on his cheek attested to his having been kicked in the face by a horse, but nothing scarred him as much as the memories of borrowed money and merciless loan companies preying on him and his burnt-out neighbours. It wasn't because he had any attachment to goods: "I wouldn't give you a chew of tobacco for a whole train load," was how he valued most things. When he first tasted tequila in Mexico, he even included Mexico in the chew. Real value, for him, lay within his family, his faith, and his community.

He wanted his family to have things in life when they needed them, but didn't want the things to be the stuff of life.

My South American research trip was held back by about two weeks, but I leave on it now with relief, knowing that my dad's trip is done. When he finished a good meal with a "cup of good strong tea," his wrist would circle the saucer with a unique little motion before he set the cup firmly down. "Thank God for that," he would say. What more could I add?

PEACE!

Roberto

Brazil

"Only the enemy has changed."

Rio remains one of the great cities of the world. I have been back several times since the letters and I have had the privilege of ushering friends through this "cidade marvilhosa" (the wonderful city) three times. In August 1989 I went back to Brazil to celebrate the 25th anniversary of our arrival in the Mission of União dos Palmares.

I had the joy of having my niece, Marianne Kebe, accompany me. She had been born in Brazil when my sister lived there, but had never been back. We were both thrilled to find the hospital where she was born in Salvador de Bahia, the church where she was baptized, and the apartment her family had lived in. I snapped her picture with three other Bahian women roughly her own age. She was as white as they were black, but they were all Bahians. As far as the Brazilian women were concerned, Marianne had the greatest privilege anybody could have. She had been born in Brazil.

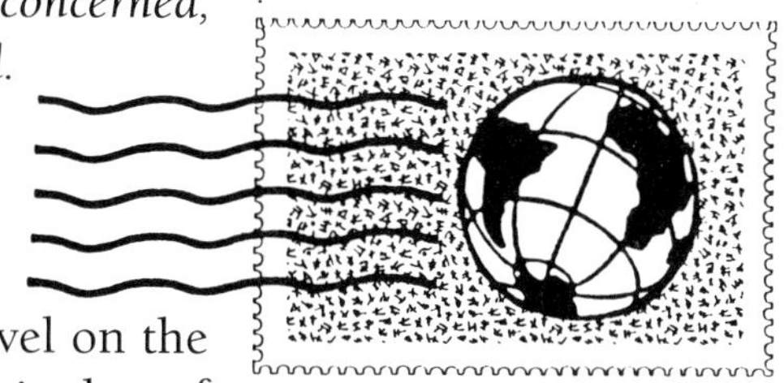

Rio de Janeiro, Brazil
September 1, 1976

Victor Alejandro Zuniga Varga is dying. He lies paralysed with a broken hip in a hovel on the slopes of a grey, stark, sandy mountain outside Lima. Victor is in his 70s. His face is that of an Inca, and his eyes are sunk deep behind his high cheekbones. His black hair has only a few streaks of white. It is stiff and has been crudely cut. His main worry is that the roof of his shack will fall in before he dies. He has reason to worry. The frail sticks that hold up the sheets of rusty tin and cardboard are ready to fall.

Grey clouds hung over the grey hill as we climbed up the garbage-strewn path to his hut. Our shoes stirred the dry dust. The only colour on the mountainside came from the tissue-paper kites which the little barefoot boys were flying in the cool breeze. I had to hunch my way into the opening that was the door. A skinny dog eyed me suspiciously. Two ducks pecked at a handful of corn in a tin can. A bony rooster was tied by a string to the leg of a chair. Victor was glad to see the Sister who brought me. So were his retarded son and his deaf old wife.

The walls of the "house" are cardboard and they are papered over with old newspapers. A headline says, "GEMINI 12 WILL RETURN TODAY!" A chorus girl's picture from a magazine cover is beneath a little framed holy picture of "Nuestro Senor de los Milagros." A piece of Blessed Palm is held up by the same nail that holds a coal-oil lantern without a glass. Piles of junk and a chamber pot are beneath the dirty old bed. The blare of a radio in a nearby dwelling fills the room.

Victor tells us of his problems. There are 13 people who live with him. Only one of his sons has a job. Victor knows that he is a "cargo"–a weight to be carried–and hopes that the

Lord will take him soon. Big tears come to his eyes and trickle down into the wrinkles when he wonders what will happen if that son loses his job. His son is one of the millions who scrape a living out of a long day's toil. He leaves early in the morning for the factory far away. It is difficult to get there. The buses have been on strike. There have been riots and demonstrations. Martial law has meant 8:00 P.M. curfews. Anyone walking out after that will be shot on sight.

Earthquake tremors are common. The mountain itself is a result of some gigantic shake in ancient times. Victor is used to the tremors. He was born in Cuzco, the old capital of the Inca Empire. He talks of his boyhood high in the Andes, how he had herded animals on the *hacienda* of the landowner. He remembers that he could catch a fish in a brook whenever he wanted. Now a fish costs 30 soles. He has only been on this mountainside for about 15 years. He was one of the hundreds of thousands who had headed for the big city to find work. They all ended up in the dark slums that surround the capital.

Down below, a steady stream of old cars and buses whizzes along the Avenida Tupa Amara, the road link between the marginalized and the rest of the people. Tupa Amara was the last of the Inca kings. He continues to be the symbol of struggle against the oppressor. A long time ago, he was captured, converted, baptized, and beheaded all in the same week. The struggle has never ceased for his people. Only the enemy has changed. There is a new language to talk about it now. A Sister said, "To transform finds its truth in the concrete reality and its revolutionary praxis in applied theory in the present." There may be an easier way of saying it, but one thing is for sure, something has to change.

The morning visit to Victor reminded me so much of another day an eon of years ago in 1964 when I first visited a *favella*, a slum, on a mountainside above Rio de Janeiro. With a number of trainees from the Cultural School in Petroposis, we had climbed that mountainside with one of our *profesoras*. Fresh out of the safety of clerical clothes and shiny shoes, the squalor of that afternoon will forever leave a deep impression on me. Ragged kids with fat bellies were flying their tiny kites in the gentle breeze that passed over the peak of the ridge. Black, hairy pigs dug in a garbage heap. Semihostile eyes squinted out from shacks at the camera-carrying gringos. Far below was the splendour of Guanabara Bay, Sugar Loaf Mountain, and Copacabana Beach. Loudspeakers blared scratchy music and steady advertisements at the favella dwellers.

I remember a little boy was crying. His mother had just struck him. I asked our profesora why. She talked to the mother and then explained to us that the little boy had used some of the water out of the earthen pot to wash his hands. The water was for cooking and drinking. The mother had started down to the tap at the bottom of the hill at 4:00 A.M. She had stood in line for three hours till she got her turn at the *charferiz*. Then she had climbed the steep mountainside in the broiling morning sun with the pot of water on her head. So much of herself had been invested in the water, that her anger had erupted when it appeared even a tiny bit was wasted.

Since then I have come to appreciate the value of water so much more. I have seen burning deserts and the skeletons of dead animals, deserted villages and dry wells, swollen bellies and dying children. I have learned to take a small swig from a little flask knowing that that was the last drinking water left for the present. Even though I grew up in a house that did not have "hot and cold running water," even though we had to buy "drinking water" at five cents for two pails, even though Saturday-night bath water went through the third and fourth use in front of the kitchen stove, it took these other kinds of experiences to make me truly appreciate the value of water.

Is it any wonder that Jesus said, "I am the Living Water?" Is it any wonder that Hindus flock to their sacred rivers to be renewed and that they have picked the Lotus, a water plant, to be the symbol of life? If Barbara Ward's suggestion at the HABITAT conference to "give clean water to everybody on the globe" were accepted and effected, it would truly be a revolutionary idea.

As well as Lima, my trip to Latin America brought me through Philadelphia and the Eucharist Congress for a few days. I spent time with Dom Helder Camara, the tiny "pacific" fighting archbishop of Recife, Brazil. It was easier to talk to him there than in his home country. It was also a chance to see the maze of different viewpoints that make up the Catholic Church today. By and large the gathering could have taken place 20 years ago . . . the same people representing the same things would have been there. Although it was supposed to be an international event, it was really an American show, another peg in the celebrations of '76. The basic theme there was world hunger. Not too many people looked hungry.

Some of the bishops who were in Philadelphia met the following week in Ecuador. They were the representatives of CELAM, the Conference of Latin American Bishops. All were arrested and expelled, along with their advisors, for being "subversives." That is a loosely used word in this part of the world, and it marks the line between the few who have and the multitude who have not. I can feel a new tension in the countries I have visited.

In Bolivia, I had my closest run-in with the Avenging Angel. I went "down for the count" with altitude sickness. At 12,000 feet I ran out of air. Fortunately, I was with some friends who got me to medical attention and oxygen, but it took several hospital days before I was mobile again, and I finished my stay there with a portable oxygen mask.

However, I did meet a kind of living legend in the mountains. A 56-year-old American known as "Padre Tex" by thousands of Bolivians, he builds roads where roads have never been built before. The son of a Rocky Mountain road-building family, he is a John Wayne type and a Son of St. Francis. He is big, rangy, and tough in his cowboy boots, blue denim shirt, and baggy pants. His Franciscan habit hangs on a nail behind a makeshift desk. His face is lined

Rio de Janeiro, Brazil

with 26 years of experience in South America and he smokes black cigars. He is poor at paperwork but great at moving mountains. "If you could pave roads with paper, we'd have 160 miles of paved roads." He's the kind of guy who gets free gas from Gulf Oil with an Athol Murray approach to God, life, and men. He uses Canadian money from CCODP to pay his crew something akin to a living wage. "It takes two years to get a crack tractor operator. There are two ways to operate – Padre Tex's way and the wrong way." Yet through it all, a kind of simple, Franciscan gentleness emerges. "What we are doing is nothing new, all the roads in South America were built by the friars and the Indians 400 years ago." Of course, the Incas built some pretty amazing roads themselves in pre-conquest days.

I have a three-month, 25-project trip ahead of me in this great land . . .

Abraços,

"This is the land where sugar is king, and where sugar is king, both people and nature suffer."

It was a great joy to return to our mission for its 25th anniversary in August 1989. How happy I was to be reunited with so many very good friends. While living there I had learned that wisdom is found in the most amazing places; rarely does one encounter it in the minds of the rich and powerful. Rather, true wisdom is the companion of those who are weak and who have suffered and are powerless.

Although the efforts made by those of us who worked at the mission are slowly passing, our presence did plant some seeds. I have always been impressed by those who are ready to take the step into the future and are not bothered by the consequences. Over the years I find that there seem to be fewer people in our culture ready to do this, and that makes me sad.

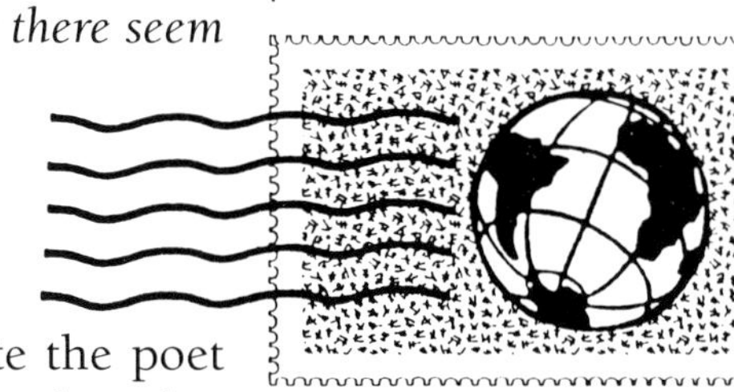

União Dos Palmares, Brazil
October 1, 1976

"Five years have passed; five summers, with the length of five long winters!" wrote the poet Wordsworth about his second visit to Tintern Abbey. I couldn't help but think similar thoughts as I worked my way north along the coast of Brazil this past month. Six years have passed since I left Brazil to return to Canada. Twelve years have gone by since I first saw the airport at Maceió. That first time we arrived in an old Constellation with worn tires. This time the flight was in a spanking new Boeing 727 with deluxe service. The old war-weary DC-3s and 4s seemed to have disappeared. I wondered who was buying the used planes from Brazil.

Canadian friends were waiting with an open-arms welcome. Palm trees were swaying in a light breeze. Puffy white clouds scudded across a clear blue sky. A new hard-top road sweeps out to União dos Palmares where the Serra de Barriga (Stomach Mountain) still stands guard over the valley. The Serra looks down over the town where I spent my six years in Brazil. It has a special place in Brazilian history, in world history for that matter, because it was there that African slaves threw off the yoke of the slave masters for the first time. For 70 years these transplanted Africans lived as free people until the Portuguese stamped out their hopes. Their cry for freedom died with their leader, Zumbi.

This is the land where sugar is king, and where sugar is king, both people and nature suffer. Forests have been ripped off the mountains to make way for cane, people have been driven off the land for the same purpose. But on the day of my arrival, the land looked beautiful. Post-winter rains had left the area as bright and green as a "golf course." Workers were beginning to hack into stalks as high as telephone poles. Sugar mills had been rebuilt and enlarged. Cars whizzed by on the road that used to be a spring-breaking, gut-stirring, mud-splashing event

Sugarcane harvest, Brazil

every time we used it. Now the drive is a few minutes of high-speed pleasure. Microwave towers indicate that there is now direct-dial, international telephone service to the whole world.

Things have really changed, or so it would seem, but in the days that I spent there I could see that little has changed for the majority of people. Undernourished children still work long hours in the cane fields. Health campaigns have been mounted but endemic diseases continue to drag great numbers into a perpetual state of ill health. Wages in no way keep up to the spiralling inflationary prices. Life for the poor was hard before. It is harder today.

The popular greeting is still, "Todo Bom?" (Everything okay?) The reply is always the same: "Todo Bom!" (Everything okay!) In this spirit, our Brazilian friends continue to confront the history that is theirs.

One of the highlights of my stay here was visiting a project that I had personally directed – the construction of the Villa Paulo VI after the disastrous floods of 1969. The 50 homes are still in use, well looked after, and in a tropical garden of fruits and flowers. The water system is working well and has been extended to the neighbourhood. Above all, I noticed that the worm-swollen bellies of the children have hardened down to healthy tummies because of pure water.

The most distressing part of my journey has been through the great drought area of central Brazil. The worst drought in living memory has turned the area into a desolate place. The following is taken from a report I am writing on the projects there. Someday it might find its way into a book.

* * * * * * * * * *

Miguel was a *vaqueiro*, a cattle driver. He loved the smell of horses, the sound of leather on leather, a fresh wind in his face, the lowing of herds at night. Today he was thirsty and hungry. He stood with his wife and children at a corner where the two roads met. Miguel looked across the road and watched a goat stand on its hind legs, lean its front feet against the trunk of a gnarled, scrubby tree, and stretch its neck out. The goat tried to nibble the few leaves that still remained on the lower branches. Other goats searched the dry dust and the stony, red earth to see if some stalk of green grass might remain.

Miguel thought, "All the cows are gone, all the sheep are gone, only the goats remain." That told how long the drought had been. The cows are the first to go. Then the sheep will die, too. Then all that are left are the people, and of course, the donkeys. People and donkeys; they always last the longest.

The sun burned down. It had been burning for a long time . . . longer in fact than anybody could remember. There had been no rain this year. Oh yes, the clouds would come. They came every day in fact, but they would pass over and the sun would continue to burn down. The wind was always blowing – a hot, dry wind with sand particles in it that stung the face. The

School built under the directi
of Father Bob

trees and bushes looked dead. The water holes had no water, just the hardened imprints of animals' feet when they had gone for the last drink. Bloated carcasses and whitened bones were scattered over the land.

High overhead the vultures circled in great arcs. This was a good time for vultures. They had plenty to eat. Most of the other birds had gone. The bare bushes held their empty nests. Birds could fly and they would find water. And near the water they would find some food.

But in the land itself, there was hunger, hunger that stretched across the burnt bush country to the purple serras. People were now eating the cacti, which grew despite the lack of rain. Miguel and his family had tried to eat some this morning. It was foul tasting and stringy, and it did not kill the hunger eating at their ribs. Their fathers and grandfathers had sometimes eaten it before, but the bitter cactus was always the last resort.

Life itself was bitter now, for the poor people at least. They stood on the roads in little groups, their faces lean and gaunt, their eyes listless. Sometimes they had a few belongings tied up in a bundle, sometimes they didn't. They would wait for a ride, for somebody to pick them up, or they would walk, their worn sandals kicking up little spirals of dust as they moved. They didn't really know which way to go, but they knew that they had to leave the land. They loved the land because it was theirs. They had no documents to prove it, but in their hearts they needed none. It was their land. They had fought it and tamed it. They loved its clear air, its blue skies, its peaceful nights. They loved the solitude . . . the quiet that made it possible to stand in awe before their God. The land had made them tough. That was why they lasted longer than the cows, and the sheep, and even the goats. They had fought the thorns and the bushes and the searing sun, and they had survived.

* * * * * * * * * *

Each season in Brazil is marked with different events. September is the month of independence, and every place I have gone, in big city or small village, there has been the sound of drum and bugle bands practising. The one universal quality that all the bands have, be they good or bad, is that they are loud. My ears keep ringing with the sound long after the instruments are hung up for the night. The national slogan this year is, "This is one country that is going forward."

Até Logo,

Family of sugarcane workers

"To earn your bread by the sweat of your brow."

Brasilia is a unique kind of city–halfway between a world fair and a garbage dump. As I was the only Portuguese-speaking member of Parliament in my days in the House, I travelled with several committees and task forces to the capital of Brazil. My trips to the developing world over the last 30 years have shown me that, if anything, the general situation has deteriorated. It is hard for me to understand why the West has almost completely ignored something of such horrible magnitude. Someday we are going to wake up and see faces in our windows. They have come to take because we are not ready to give. This lack of understanding of what is going on in the world was the main reason behind founding Broadcasting for International Understanding.

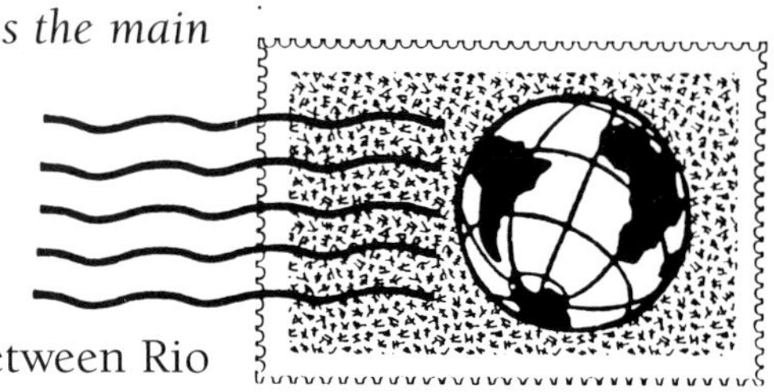

Brasilia, Brazil
November 1, 1976

Over a month ago, a powerful black car sped through the night on the main road between Rio and São Paulo. Nobody will ever know what really happened. It seems the car tried to pass a bus, went out of control, jumped the dividing barrier, and was demolished by an oncoming truck. The driver and passenger died on the spot. The passenger was one of the legends of the modern world, Juscelino Kubitschek, former president of Brazil.

Hundreds of thousands turned out for his funeral. He was buried in Brasilia and rightly so, for this city was his brain child. In the late 1950s, Kubitschek used the building of this modern capital as bait to draw people into the interior of the country. He personally selected a site in the high, red, prairie bush-land of the state of Goias where the sky is an exquisite blue and the climate has a perpetual springlike quality. Overcoming every kind of imaginable opposition, he brought his dream to an irreversible reality before he left office after his five-year term. In 1960, on my first visit to Brazil, an American businessman in Rio remarked, "When the USA wanted people to move west, they didn't move Washington to Denver; they built a railroad." At that time, old DC-3s were flying cement more than 500 miles to the construction site. There was no railroad and no highway. Now all that has changed, of course.

In the revolution of 1964, Kubitschek and many others of similar leanings lost their political rights. He spent 10 years in exile in Europe. At his funeral, the people carrying his body to the cemetery sang a popular folk song that he had loved: "How can the fish live outside the water . . . he can't, any more than I can live without you."

Brasilia is still under construction. New embassies, supermarkets, apartment blocks, clubs, and government offices gobble up all available cement, bricks, and lumber. Labour lives in five surrounding satellite cities. Brasilia itself is shaped like a giant airplane flying over the city's artificial lake. When the north wing is finished, it will be necessary to go back and reconstruct the south. The place still has a kind of campground feel to it. It doesn't seem real. It is almost as if it could be packed up and moved to the next world fair. Nearly a million human beings are living here now. It will be up to them to create the soul.

For a good part of the last month, I have worked my way along the north coast of Brazil and up the Amazon River. A long-time Brazilian priest friend from near União dos Palmares has travelled most of the route with me. There have been plenty of slow boats, vicious mosquitoes, interesting people and hot, humid days . . .

. . . As I was drinking the hot, strong, black coffee, I realized that I was the only one present who could appreciate the problem of the Japanese who had prepared the English instructions on the back of the large thermos bottle. They read:

> CAUTION: 1) Do not shake the pot until getting warm inner glass when boiling water being insided.
> 2) Do not overturn the pot to avoid breakage inner glass.
> 3) Take care for children's treatment.

The instructions didn't change the taste of the coffee, the welcome of the people, or the heat of the day.

It had only been a few minutes since we had skimmed in over the tops of the coconut palms. The rented Cessna Skylane with full flaps down bounced on the short runway, sent flocks of birds scurrying, and turned around just before we ran out of gravel strip.

The morning papers, being read by everyone at the Belem airclub before we had taken off, announced in heavy, black headlines: EVERYONE DEAD ON PLANE WHICH CRASHED ON MARAJO. A full-spread aerial photo showed the remnants of the plane scattered over the green carpet of jungle. Our pilot, in true Brazilian style, had informed us as we taxied out that they had never lost two planes on two consecutive days. He was in his 40s, had a clean white shirt, and a slight smell of last night's beer on his breath. He flew the airplane as if he were a part of it, and his prophecy proved true. He brought us safely to Marajó, a great nation-sized island in the mouth of the Amazon. When we landed we were less than one-half degree south of *paralelo zero* . . . the equator.

We were met by a 50-year-old Italian lady volunteer. She was a nurse, a bit on the chunky side, who had spent 10 years on the island and believed in justice for the poor. She was cross-eyed, wore dark glasses, and was wrinkled from the water and sun. She was full-busted, had a semimilitary-style red shirt, a plaid skirt with a broken zipper, floppy sandals, and a voice like a drill sergeant. If Mussolini had had more like her, Montgomery would not have had a chance in the desert.

Our transport was the only vehicle in the region, a 40-year-old army truck, a "gift" from the people of Switzerland. It was camouflaged, dual-tired, with the heavy, upright, squared appearance of the early 1930s. The steering wheel was on the right-hand side. There was a duplicate set of hand and foot controls, wooden floor boards, and directions everywhere in German and French. As we climbed in, I felt like we were getting ready to shoot a rerun of "For Whom the Bell Tolls."

My friends and I got in on the left side, our nurse friend on the right. This left the skinny, dark-skinned driver squeezed between us. He drove with care over the trails which had been built by the local cooperative community. He had to. The nearest replacement parts for the truck were in some museum in Europe.

As my year of study with the International Development Research Centre runs down to the end, I am trying to sort out in my mind all the people, experiences, places that have been part of it. It will not be easy, and in the end there will be just one more bias about development. But I do think that there should be some stories worth telling.

I think one of my most lasting memories will be the act of sweating. "To earn your bread by the sweat of your brow," was the way Genesis said it. To sweat, whether you are earning your bread or not, is a real part of the human condition. For a good period of this month, that has been my major job . . . sweating great quantities of body juice. The human system in its fight to keep cool uses the basic physics of water evaporation. In more frigid climes, our personal thermostats keep our body heat at more or less an even keel with short bursts of refrigeration. This happens when one overexerts. But in the Amazon Valley and places like it, where the heat covers you day and night, like a rubber blanket, enveloping everything, one sweats all the time. The local people adapt. They always look shiny. They have a constant film of liquid keeping them more or less comfortable, but the visitor still cools himself in spurts. One of the first expressions that a foreigner learns in Brazil is, "Uma brahma chopp, bem gelada." . . . A bottle of beer, very cold.

Mail has been scarce in Brazil, viu?

Abraços,

Roberto

Sunset in Brazil

"But a camera still fascinates me . . . A one-and-only smile, an insect, a flower, a group of friends, a sunset, a cloud, a happening is yours to relive another day."

People often ask me where my home is. I tell them it is where I hang my cap, and that's the truth. I know that any day could be my last, and I want to be at home no matter where it happens. But if I had a choice I would make it Saskatchewan, for it was here I discovered that the horizon is always in sight. There are no insurmountable hills in between. This idea has been a great advantage to me in life. No mountain is impossible to cross. Just make it until tomorrow and there will be a new horizon.

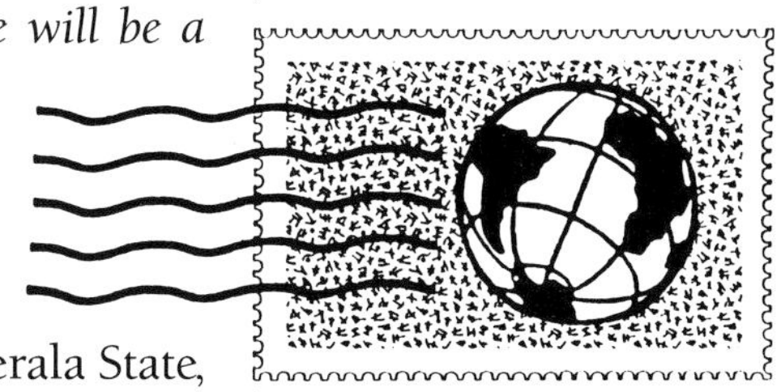

Saskatchewan
December 1, 1976

Battleford, Rome, Paris, Vimy Ridge, Riviére Qui Barre, Varadero, Ottawa, New Delhi, Kerala State, Calcutta, International Date Line, Montreal, flying down to Rio, Rio de Janeiro, União dos Palmares, Brasilia, and finally Saskatchewan, again. These have been the date lines of my news notes during the past 15 months of study and research. This will be the last in the series, for there is a time for travelling and a time for stopping.

All in all, it has been a unique and wonderful experience, one that I have tried to share to some extent with you through these notes. I have found my year with the International Development Research Centre one of the best of my life. I appreciate, to an extent that I cannot fully express, the openness and freedom that marks their relationship with their Associate Award Winners. There are many other areas of today's ecclesiastical, academic, and business world that could copy their style.

I date-line this Saskatchewan because as yet I do not know what my immediate future holds. But Saskatchewan is home base, and no matter where one goes, if he has grown up in gumbo soil, he has a special affinity for the mud of this earth. Black mud, grey mud, yellow mud, red mud . . . I've tramped all kinds. However, this year, if I was to give a general impression of weather, I would say, "drought." I spent more time in burnt-out lands than in wet areas. Water, or rather lack of it, has been a haunting reality in most of the lands I visited.

My trip to Ottawa from Brazil was made up of five airplanes, five stopovers, 30 hours of travel, a temperature change from the high 90s to below freezing, and the beginnings of a cold.

Upon returning there were a series of interviews and talks, visits to various funding agencies, and a checkup at the tropical disease hospital. This means checking everything that one is "voiding." Parasites, bugs, worms, and beasties that have been picked up in the tropics all receive special treatment. The treatment generally amounts to pill and void, check and re-pill. There are probably other medical terms to cover the treatment involved. Actually, I was incredibly fortunate to have gone so far through such bad conditions without having to spend time in hospitals. My only medical encounter was when the high altitude of the Andes unexpectedly pulled the rug out from under my feet.

I left Brazil on the 15th of November. On that day, the country was in the throes of a national election at the municipal level. I had been through the long, agonizing, and often brutal campaigning that preceded it. When I arrived in Montreal, the passenger in front of me was told by the immigration officer, "Tomorrow is the first day of a new era." Only then did I realize that Quebec was having an election. Brazilian newspapers had somehow missed it. Canadians realized that Réné Lévesque is one of the best political organizers in the land, and that "separatism" is no longer a bad word, but a possibility. Many problems still remain: for instance, "What will they call the Montreal Canadiens after separation?"

Later in the week, I went down to the National War Memorial to use up the end of a film I had started in the tropics. The grey, snow-laden, November clouds hung low over the city. The war memorial blended into the dull days of late autumn. Suddenly there was the patter of little feet, the babble of cherry-cheeked youngsters, the bright red, blue, green, purple, pink mish-mash of snowsuits, toques, parkas, and scarves of a grade four class. Lines were formed at the base of the monument and I could see the breath of the children as they sang, "O Canada, terre de nos aïeux . . ." Like all good Canadians they didn't know the second verse of the national anthem. When I left them, the teachers had let them climb up onto the monument, and the frozen, black, metal figures of soldiers, sailors, pilots, nurses, cannons, and muddy boots were alive with the colours of children in the winter.

For those who took a few minutes at times to drop me a letter or note while I was on safari, I want to say a public word of thanks to you. There is really nothing like a message from someone who cares. There are many things which work against letter writing, I suppose. The insecurity of the postal service is one thing. Telephones and more rapid transport all have something to do with it, but most of all I think it is the loss of a habit. To me this is a tragedy, because I still think that the skill of good letter writing is a great art.

I can well remember waiting for my mother's letters while I was studying at the seminary. Long before that, I can still see her, straight pen in hand with a yellow, smoky coal-oil lamp that shed a shaky shadow around the winter quarters of our prairie home. Thick layers of frost blotted out the window and a "Quebec" heater battled against the inroads of a sweeping blizzard through the uninsulated walls. She wrote about the simple things and made them new and interesting: the laundry, the chickens, the dog, the neighbour's visit, the coyote's howling, the garden, a child's sniffles, the drought, "relief," codfish. The letters were sent to the folks "down east," to a soldier somewhere in England, to a neighbour sick in the hospital. And for a moment somebody would have a better day.

A long chapter could be written about the mail service that I have seen this year. The Indian mail service is the best in the world . . . bar none. In the cities, five mail deliveries a day, seven pickups, six days a week. It is cheap, quick, and sure. The Indians have merely retained the old British system of the 1890s which had several basic principles: a) Mail is important; b) The mail must go through; c) To be a postman is a good thing. On the other hand the great maze of inefficiency that was the Brazilian system has been straightened out somewhat in the last few years. It has been taken over by a private organization. New bright yellow uniforms, trucks, mailboxes, and stamps make the external look good. Brazilians still run the system and therein lies the catch. A letter, to a Brazilian, is a rare thing, a precious thing, a thing that generally says nothing except, "I am remembering you. I hope that you are well. We are all well here." Whether this message comes today or tomorrow is incidental. Letters are never discarded. They are a little bit of the other person, so they are kept. The Canadian system, if system it is, is beyond comment or description.

A long time ago, in June 1964, outside the Cathedral of Milan, Italy, thieves broke up what was otherwise a pleasant day for my father, sister, and I. They stole our rented car, our baggage, our plane tickets, our money, and my passport. By some quirk of fate, I had my camera in my hand, so *it*, at least, did not increase the national income of Italy for that year. It has remained a kind of symbol to me because everything else was gone. My father's remark at the time, "A few bags don't mean much if you have been hailed out three times in your life," seemed inadequate. I understand it better now.

But a camera still fascinates me. All you have to do is set it at the right speed, find the right lens opening, point it in the right direction, at the right distance and the right time and *snap*—a section of life, of nature, of creation is captured. A one-and-only smile, an insect, a flower, a group of friends, a sunset, a cloud, a happening is yours to relive another day. I took about 1,000 slides during the past year. A few of them aren't bad . . . in fact, some of them are damn good.

My past experience in returning from foreign countries has been a kind of reverse culture shock. I expect it again. Christmas is not really a good time to come back from hungry people. At no other time of the year is the absurdity of abundance so clear. Useless gifts for those who need no gifts. Great gobs of food for those who already eat and drink too much. But that's the way it is.

And yet at the same time, the Christmas story is still real—the total gift of self, of "losing" all for the other, of leaving behind all that is safe, and dying. And in this dying and leaving behind, peace will come. And my sincerest wish and prayer for each and every one is that you will find that kind of peace.

Até Deus quiser . . .
Until the Lord wills it,

Roberto

Brazil

I wish to acknowledge and thank
Br. Louis O.M.I. *of North Battleford, Sask.,*
my sister Mary Lou, and Charlene Dobmeier, both of Saskatoon, Sask.
for their contribution of photographs.